MASTERING CHANGE

Marie Tongs

Copyright © 2024 Marie Tongs
Mastering Change

All rights reserved. No part of this publication may be reproduced, transmitted, or stored in a retrieval system in any form or by any means, without permission in writing from the copyright holder.

Published in Nigeria in 2024 by Plexity Digital

A catalogue record of this book will be available from the National Library of Nigeria.

TABLE OF CONTENTS

FOREWORD iv
INTRODUCTION v

CHAPTER ONE: MASTERING CHANGE 1

CHAPTER TWO: NAVIGATING UNCERTAINTY IN A RAPIDLY CHANGING MARKET 11

CHAPTER THREE: THE POWER OF AGILITY IN ENTERPRISE LEADERSHIP 23

CHAPTER FOUR: LIFELONG LEARNING IN A COMPETITIVE BUSINESS ENVIRONMENT 35

CHAPTER FIVE: THE BUSINESS IMPACT OF EMERGING TECHNOLOGIES AND MARKET SHFTS 51

CHAPTER SIX: THE FUTURE OF WORK LEADING IN AN ERA OF TRANSFORMATION 68

CHAPTER SEVEN: ETHICAL CHALLENGES IN A CHANGING BUSINESS LANDSCAPE 84

CHAPTER EIGHT: THE ROLE OF CLOUD, AI, AND DIGITAL INFRASTRUCTURE IN BUSINESS EVOLUTION 100

CHAPTER NINE: FROM LEGACY SYSTEM TO INTELLIGENT AUTOMATION 118

CHAPTER TEN: BUILDING A FUTURE-PROOF CAREER IN A CONSTANTLY EVOLVING BUSINESS WORLD 137

FOREWORD

Change is not just a force in business, it is the foundation of innovation, growth, and long-term success. Across industries, organizations that master change thrive, while those resistant to it risk stagnation. From shifts in consumer behavior to the rapid advancement of technology, the ability to adapt is what separates market leaders from those left behind.

This book, *Mastering Change*, is not about resisting disruption; it's about embracing it as a competitive advantage. It is a guide for business leaders, entrepreneurs, and professionals who want to navigate uncertainty, seize new opportunities, and turn challenges into catalysts for transformation.

You will gain insights into the strategies that future-proof organizations, the mindsets that drive innovation, and the leadership qualities that foster resilience. Whether you are leading a multinational corporation, launching a startup, or managing organizational change, this book provides the tools to make agility your strongest asset.

Change is inevitable, but mastering it is a choice. This book will show you how.

INTRODUCTION

Change in business is not just frequent, it's relentless. What once defined success can quickly become outdated as industries shift, technologies advance, and market dynamics evolve. The ability to navigate change isn't just an advantage—it's a necessity.

Mastering Change is a book designed for business leaders, entrepreneurs, and professionals who want to stay ahead in an era where adaptability is as critical as expertise. This book is not just about adopting new strategies; it's about developing a mindset that allows you to anticipate shifts, embrace uncertainty, and turn disruption into opportunity.

Throughout this book, we'll explore how top executives, industry pioneers, and forward-thinking organizations thrive in an environment of constant evolution. We'll discuss the frameworks that allow businesses to remain competitive, the strategies companies use to pivot successfully, and the leadership qualities that separate those who drive change from those who struggle to keep up.

By the end of this journey, you won't just react to change, you'll master it. Whether you're leading a multinational corporation, scaling a startup, or managing organizational transformation, this book will equip you with the insights and tools to future-proof your business and lead with confidence.

CHAPTER ONE
MASTERING CHANGE

Change is not an occasional event in business—it is the fundamental reality of the corporate world. From shifting market dynamics and disruptive technologies to evolving customer expectations and regulatory landscapes, businesses must navigate a landscape that never stands still. Mastering change is not just about survival; it is about positioning organizations for long-term success in an environment where adaptability is the key differentiator.

The Mindset for Mastering Change

a. Embracing a Growth Mindset

The most successful business leaders and organizations understand that change is an opportunity, not a threat. Mastering change requires the ability to learn, unlearn, and relearn—staying ahead by challenging old assumptions, embracing innovation, and continuously developing new competencies. Leaders who foster a culture of curiosity and adaptability within their teams create organizations that thrive in uncertainty.

b. Staying Agile in a Shifting Landscape

Business agility is no longer optional; it is a necessity. Companies must be able to pivot quickly in response to market disruptions, technological advancements, and competitive pressures. Agility means rethinking traditional business models, encouraging cross-functional collaboration, and ensuring that decision-making is swift, informed, and responsive to real-time data.

c. Leveraging Emerging Tools and Technologies

The rapid pace of technological innovation—ranging from automation and AI to digital transformation and blockchain—is reshaping industries. Organizations that master change do not merely adopt new technologies; they strategically integrate them to enhance efficiency, customer experience, and decision-making. Understanding when and how to implement these advancements separates market leaders from those left behind.

d. Navigating Regulatory and Ethical Shifts

Global regulations, compliance requirements, and ethical considerations are evolving just as fast as business models. Companies that proactively address issues such as data privacy, sustainability, and corporate governance position themselves for long-term trust and credibility. Mastering change means staying ahead of compliance challenges while embedding ethical decision-making into the fabric of corporate strategy.

The Path Forward: From Disruption to Opportunity

Change in business is inevitable, but those who learn to master it will lead industries, drive innovation, and create lasting value. Organizations that embrace change as a core competency will not only survive disruption but will harness it as a catalyst for growth. The key is not just to react to change but to anticipate it, shape it, and use it as a competitive advantage in an increasingly unpredictable world.

The Evolution of Business in a Disruptive World

Change has always been a defining characteristic of business. From the industrial revolution to the digital age, enterprises have had to adapt to shifts in technology, consumer behavior, and global markets. However, the pace of change today is faster than ever, driven by digital transformation, economic volatility, and evolving workforce dynamics. Business leaders who master change are not only surviving these shifts but thriving by proactively embracing innovation, agility, and resilience.

a. The Industrial Age to the Digital Era: Lessons in Adaptation

Historically, businesses that failed to adapt to change were left behind. The industrial revolution reshaped manufacturing, automation redefined efficiency, and the digital age revolutionized communication and commerce. Companies like Kodak and Blockbuster serve as cautionary tales—leaders in their industries who resisted change and were ultimately displaced by disruptive competitors. In contrast, businesses like Amazon, Apple, and

Microsoft continuously evolved, leveraging change as an opportunity rather than a threat.

b. The Shift from Traditional to Agile Leadership

The traditional top-down leadership model is no longer sufficient in an era of rapid change. Today's business leaders must be agile, making data-driven decisions while remaining flexible in strategy execution. The most successful executives foster a culture of continuous learning, encourage innovation, and empower teams to adapt quickly. Leadership in the modern business environment is about guiding organizations through uncertainty, embracing disruption, and turning challenges into opportunities.

c. Technology as a Catalyst for Transformation

The rise of artificial intelligence, automation, and cloud computing has fundamentally altered how businesses operate. Digital transformation is no longer optional, it is a necessity for survival. Companies that integrate emerging technologies to streamline operations, enhance customer experiences, and drive innovation are positioning themselves for long-term success. Mastering technological change means staying ahead of industry trends, investing in digital capabilities, and fostering a culture of adaptability.

d. Navigating Economic and Market Disruptions

Uncertainty is a constant in the business world. Economic downturns, geopolitical tensions, and supply chain disruptions create challenges that require strategic foresight and resilience. Organizations that master change build agility into their business models, diversify revenue streams, and develop contingency plans to weather economic storms. The ability to anticipate market shifts and respond proactively sets successful enterprises apart from those that struggle to keep up.

e. The Future of Work: Rethinking Organizational Agility

The workforce landscape is undergoing a significant transformation. Remote work, automation, and the gig economy are reshaping how businesses structure their teams and operations. Organizations that embrace flexible work models, prioritize employee well-being, and invest in continuous learning will remain competitive in the changing world of work. Mastering change in workforce management means adopting policies that attract and retain top talent while ensuring that organizations remain adaptable to evolving employee expectations and technological advancements.

The Rapid Shift from Traditional Business Analytics to AI-Driven Decision-Making

Change is no longer a periodic event in business; it is a constant. Organizations that once relied on traditional analytics and human intuition must now adapt to AI-driven insights, automation, and predictive analytics to stay competitive. The shift from descriptive reporting to prescriptive decision-making is transforming industries, requiring leaders to master change rather than react to it.

a. From Historical Analysis to Real-Time Strategy

Traditional business analytics focused on historical data—what happened and why. Today, AI enables real-time decision-making, allowing businesses to forecast trends, mitigate risks, and seize opportunities faster than ever. Leaders who master change understand the power of predictive and prescriptive analytics, ensuring their organizations remain proactive rather than reactive.

b. AI as a Competitive Advantage

Machine learning and AI have reshaped how businesses approach growth and efficiency. Instead of relying solely on human expertise, organizations now leverage AI to identify market trends, automate operations, and personalize customer experiences. Mastering change means knowing when and how to integrate AI for maximum impact while maintaining human oversight.

c. Navigating the Challenges of AI Adoption

While AI offers transformative potential, business leaders must address challenges such as data privacy, ethical concerns, and algorithmic bias. Companies that fail to implement AI responsibly risk reputational damage and regulatory penalties. Mastering change requires balancing innovation with governance, ensuring AI-driven decisions align with organizational values and compliance standards.

The Rise of Automation and Its Impact on Business

Automation has become a driving force in modern enterprises, streamlining operations, reducing costs, and improving productivity. However, the widespread adoption of AI-driven automation also presents challenges that business leaders must navigate carefully.

a. Embracing Automation for Efficiency and Growth

From robotic process automation (RPA) in finance to AI-powered customer service chatbots, businesses are leveraging automation to enhance efficiency. Organizations that master change recognize automation as a tool for growth rather than a threat, reallocating human capital to high-value tasks while optimizing operational workflows.

b. Workforce Transformation and the Future of Jobs

As automation takes over routine tasks, business leaders must rethink workforce strategies. Instead of replacing employees, mastering change involves reskilling and upskilling teams to work alongside AI. The future of work lies in collaboration between human expertise and intelligent systems, fostering innovation while maintaining workforce agility.

c. Ethical AI and Responsible Automation

Automating decisions at scale raises ethical concerns, from biased algorithms to job displacement. Forward-thinking organizations embed ethical considerations into AI adoption, ensuring transparency, fairness, and accountability. Business leaders who master change prioritize responsible AI frameworks, safeguarding both their brand and their stakeholders.

Leading Through Change: Strategies for Business Success

To thrive in an era of disruption, business professionals must develop a proactive approach to change management. Success depends on the ability to anticipate shifts, adapt strategies, and foster a culture of continuous innovation.

a. Cultivating an Adaptive Leadership Mindset

Leaders who excel in navigating change embrace a growth mindset, continuously learning and evolving with technological advancements. They encourage curiosity, agility, and resilience within their teams, ensuring their organizations remain competitive in fast-moving markets.

b. Implementing Scalable Digital Transformation

Digital transformation is not a one-time initiative, it's an ongoing process. Mastering change means integrating AI and automation strategically, aligning digital investments with long-term business objectives, and scaling transformation efforts without disrupting core operations.

c. Balancing Innovation with Risk Management

While innovation drives competitive advantage, unchecked experimentation can lead to costly failures. Successful leaders assess risks, implement pilot programs, and measure outcomes before full-scale deployment. Mastering change requires balancing bold innovation with pragmatic risk management.

Why Adaptability is the New Competitive Edge

The business landscape is evolving at an unprecedented pace. Strategies, technologies, and market dynamics that were once considered cutting-edge quickly become outdated. In this environment, the most valuable asset for business leaders and organizations isn't just expertise, it's adaptability.

Enterprises that embrace continuous learning, experimentation, and innovation are the ones that thrive. Disruptive technologies, shifting consumer behaviors, and evolving regulatory landscapes demand that leaders pivot, upskill, and rethink traditional approaches. Those who resist change risk losing relevance, while those who proactively adapt gain a decisive competitive advantage.

Adaptability in business goes beyond adopting new tools or technologies. It requires a shift in mindset—being open to new ways of thinking, integrating cross-functional insights, and refining strategies based on real-world feedback. Organizations must move away from rigid, long-term plans and embrace more dynamic, agile decision-making that evolves with market conditions.

In a world where data-driven insights and digital transformation define success, adaptability isn't just an advantage—it's a necessity. Businesses that cultivate a culture of continuous learning, encourage innovation, and empower their teams with the agility to navigate disruption will not only survive but lead in the future of enterprise.

CHAPTER TWO
NAVIGATING UNCERTAINTY IN A RAPIDLY CHANGING MARKET

Change is no longer a periodic disruption—it is the defining reality of modern business. Markets shift overnight, customer expectations evolve, and emerging technologies upend traditional business models. In this environment, uncertainty is not a challenge to be avoided but a force to be mastered. The most successful business leaders are those who embrace uncertainty, anticipate disruption, and turn volatility into a competitive advantage.

1. The Nature of Uncertainty in Business

Uncertainty in today's market comes from multiple sources—economic fluctuations, geopolitical shifts, rapid technological advancements, and changing consumer behavior. Traditional planning models based on stability are no longer sufficient. To succeed, businesses must develop a proactive approach to uncertainty that prioritizes agility, innovation, and resilience.

2. Developing an Adaptive Business Strategy

Rigid, long-term strategic plans often fail in volatile markets. Instead, organizations must adopt adaptive strategies that allow for quick pivots and course corrections. This requires:

    i. Scenario Planning – Anticipating multiple future possibilities and preparing responses for each.

    ii. Data-Driven Decision Making – Leveraging real-time insights to make informed, agile decisions.

    iii. Cross-Functional Agility – Encouraging collaboration across departments to respond rapidly to market changes.

3. Leveraging Technology to Stay Ahead

Technology is both a driver of uncertainty and a tool for managing it. Businesses that integrate AI, automation, and data analytics into their operations gain a significant advantage. Key areas of focus include:

    i. Predictive Analytics – Using data to anticipate market shifts before they happen.

    ii. AI-Powered Automation – Streamlining operations to improve efficiency and responsiveness.

    iii. Digital Transformation – Adapting to new technologies that enhance customer experiences and operational resilience.

4. Building Organizational Resilience

Resilient organizations don't just survive change—they thrive in it. Leaders must foster a culture that embraces continuous learning, adaptability, and innovation. This means:

i. Empowering Employees – Encouraging a mindset of experimentation and problem-solving.

ii. Failing Fast, Learning Faster – Viewing setbacks as opportunities for rapid iteration and improvement.

iii. Maintaining Financial and Operational Flexibility – Creating buffer zones that allow businesses to absorb shocks without compromising long-term growth.

5. Turning Uncertainty into Opportunity

The ability to master change separates market leaders from those left behind. By cultivating adaptability, leveraging technology, and fostering resilience, businesses can transform uncertainty into a source of innovation and strategic advantage. The future will always be uncertain—but those who embrace change will define it.

Understanding the Drivers of Market Uncertainty

In today's fast-paced business environment, uncertainty is the only constant. Market disruptions can arise from various sources—economic shifts, technological advancements, geopolitical tensions, and evolving consumer behaviors. Organizations that recognize and understand these factors can build resilience, mitigate risks, and capitalize on emerging opportunities.

1. Economic and Geopolitical Forces

i. Global financial fluctuations, inflation, and supply chain disruptions can create widespread uncertainty.

ii. Trade wars, sanctions, and regulatory changes impact international business operations.

iii. downturns and recessions force businesses to rethink strategies and optimize costs.

2. Technological Disruptions and Digital Transformation

i. The rapid adoption of AI, automation, and cloud computing is reshaping industries.

ii. Cybersecurity risks and data privacy concerns are increasing as businesses digitize operations.

iii. Legacy businesses struggle to compete with tech-driven startups and digital-native enterprises.

3. Changing Consumer Expectations and Market Behavior

i. Customers demand hyper-personalization, seamless digital experiences, and ethical business practices.

ii. social media and influencer marketing rapidly shift brand loyalty and purchasing trends.

iii. E-commerce, subscription models, and the gig economy redefine traditional business structures.

4. Industry-Specific Disruptions and Competitor Movements

i. Market leaders who fail to innovate risk being displaced by agile competitors.

ii. Industry consolidation, mergers, and acquisitions reshape competitive landscapes.

iii. Regulatory changes can create new barriers or open opportunities for market expansion.

Turning Uncertainty into Opportunity

Instead of reacting to change, businesses must proactively anticipate and prepare for it. Companies that invest in data-driven insights, strategic agility, and a culture of continuous innovation will be best positioned to thrive in an uncertain world.

Strategic Adaptation: Preparing for the Unknown

Uncertainty in business is not a temporary challenge—it's a permanent reality. The most successful enterprises are those that anticipate, adapt, and innovate in response to change. Strategic adaptation is not about reacting to disruptions but about developing proactive frameworks to thrive in an unpredictable environment.

1. Building an Agile Decision-Making Framework

i. Move from rigid, long-term planning to dynamic, scenario-based strategies.

ii. Foster a culture of adaptability, empowering teams to respond quickly to change.

iii. data-driven decision-making, using real-time insights to guide business strategies.

2. Strengthening Organizational Resilience

i. Develop risk management strategies to mitigate potential threats before they escalate.

ii. Diversify revenue streams and supply chains to reduce dependency on single sources.

iii. Create contingency plans for economic downturns, regulatory shifts, and market disruptions.

3. Leveraging Innovation for Competitive Advantage

i. Invest in emerging technologies like AI, automation, and cloud solutions to stay ahead.

ii. Encourage cross-functional collaboration to drive creative problem-solving.

iii. Embrace experimental business models, testing new approaches in controlled environments.

4. Cultivating a Future-Ready Workforce

i. continuous learning programs to upskill employees for evolving roles.

ii. Foster leadership adaptability, ensuring executives can navigate uncertainty with confidence.

iii. a growth mindset, where change is seen as an opportunity rather than a threat.

Mastering Change Through Strategic Adaptation

The ability to prepare for the unknown is what separates resilient businesses from vulnerable ones. By embedding agility, resilience, and innovation into their DNA, companies can turn uncertainty into an opportunity for transformation and growth.

In today's volatile business landscape, disruption is no longer an exception, it is the norm. From economic downturns and geopolitical shifts to rapid technological advancements and evolving consumer expectations, businesses must navigate a landscape of continuous change. The organizations that thrive are those that recognize change not as a threat but as a catalyst for reinvention.

Embracing Agility as a Core Business Strategy

Agility is more than a buzzword—it is a mindset that enables companies to pivot quickly in response to market shifts. Organizations that embed agility into their strategy are better positioned to anticipate challenges, experiment with new models, and make data-driven decisions in real time. Agile businesses operate with a growth mindset, encouraging teams to iterate, learn, and adapt without fear of failure.

Resilience: Strengthening the Business Core

Resilience is the foundation of long-term success. It is not just about surviving disruptions but about emerging stronger from them. Companies that prioritize resilience invest in robust risk management frameworks, financial stability, and a culture of adaptability. They build systems that can withstand shocks—whether it's supply chain disruptions, regulatory changes, or unexpected economic downturns.

Innovation as a Driver of Sustainable Growth

Innovation is no longer optional—it is a survival imperative. Companies that master change do not just react to industry shifts; they drive them. By fostering a culture of continuous innovation, businesses can stay ahead of competitors, create new revenue streams, and deliver value in novel ways. This requires a commitment to research and development, cross-functional collaboration, and leveraging emerging technologies to unlock new possibilities.

The Roadmap to Strategic Adaptation

Mastering change through strategic adaptation requires a structured approach:

i. Scanning the Environment: Stay ahead of industry trends, competitor movements, and technological advancements.

> **ii. Scenario Planning:** Prepare for multiple potential futures by developing flexible strategies that can pivot as needed.

iii. Empowering Leadership: Equip leaders with the skills to drive change, inspire teams, and make swift yet informed decisions.

iv. Investing in Talent and Technology: Build a workforce and infrastructure that can evolve with the business landscape.

In an era defined by uncertainty, businesses that embrace change with strategic foresight will not only survive—they will lead. The future belongs to those who master change, turning disruption into a competitive advantage.

Leveraging Data and Predictive Insights for Stability

In an era of uncertainty, businesses that harness the power of data gain a crucial advantage. Predictive insights allow organizations to anticipate market shifts, customer behavior, and operational risks before they become disruptive. By integrating data-driven decision-making into their strategy, enterprises can create more resilient business models that adapt to change rather than react to it.

Companies today have access to vast amounts of structured and unstructured data, but the true challenge lies in transforming this data into actionable intelligence. Advanced analytics, artificial intelligence, and machine learning offer businesses the ability to detect trends, mitigate risks, and optimize operations with precision. Whether forecasting supply chain disruptions, identifying emerging customer demands, or managing financial risks, data-driven organizations remain a step ahead of their competitors.

Beyond internal operations, predictive insights also enable businesses to create personalized customer experiences. Enterprises that leverage behavioral analytics can anticipate needs, refine their offerings, and foster long-term customer loyalty. This level of agility ensures that companies don't just survive change but thrive within it.

To fully capitalize on data and predictive analytics, businesses must cultivate a culture of data literacy across all levels. Decision-makers need to trust and understand data-driven insights, ensuring that intuition is complemented—not replaced—by analytical precision. By embedding predictive intelligence into their strategic playbook, enterprises can move beyond reactive decision-making and establish themselves as industry leaders in a rapidly changing world.

Turning Uncertainty into a Competitive Advantage

Uncertainty is often viewed as a risk, but for forward-thinking businesses, it represents an opportunity. The most successful enterprises are those that transform unpredictability into a strategic advantage by embracing adaptability, innovation, and proactive decision-making. Rather than being paralyzed by change, these organizations use it as a catalyst for growth, positioning themselves ahead of competitors who struggle to keep up.

Shifting from Reactive to Proactive Strategies

Traditional businesses often respond to uncertainty with defensive strategies—cutting costs, reducing risk exposure, and maintaining the status quo. However, leading enterprises take a proactive approach by anticipating potential disruptions and positioning themselves to benefit from change. This includes identifying emerging market trends, experimenting with new business models, and staying ahead of regulatory or technological shifts.

Leveraging Data-Driven Decision-Making

Uncertainty can be mitigated through the intelligent use of data. Businesses that invest in analytics, artificial intelligence, and predictive modeling can gain valuable insights into market dynamics, customer behaviors, and potential risks. By making informed decisions based on real-time data, organizations can turn unpredictability into a strategic tool rather than a roadblock.

Building a Culture of Experimentation and Agility

Companies that thrive in uncertainty foster a culture of continuous learning and experimentation. They encourage employees to take calculated risks, test new ideas, and pivot quickly based on results. By treating uncertainty as an opportunity to innovate rather than a challenge to fear, businesses can uncover new revenue streams, improve operational efficiency, and differentiate themselves in the market.

Seizing First-Mover Advantage

Periods of uncertainty often create gaps in the market—gaps that agile businesses can exploit before their competitors do. Whether it's adopting a new technology, entering an emerging market, or redefining industry standards, businesses that act swiftly can establish themselves as market leaders. Instead of waiting for clarity, they embrace ambiguity as a chance to set the direction for the industry.

The Formula for Competitive Advantage in Uncertain Times

a. Monitor Industry Signals: Stay informed about economic shifts, emerging competitors, and disruptive innovations.

b. Invest in Future-Ready Capabilities: Develop workforce skills, upgrade technology infrastructure, and foster a mindset of continuous improvement.

c. Encourage Bold Leadership: Leaders must cultivate confidence in their teams by promoting calculated risk-taking and resilience.

d. Embrace Change as an Asset: View uncertainty not as a liability but as a strategic opportunity to redefine the market landscape.

By mastering change and leveraging uncertainty to their advantage, businesses can transform volatility into a springboard for success. The organizations that learn to navigate disruption with confidence and agility will be the ones that shape the future.

CHAPTER THREE
THE POWER OF AGILITY IN ENTERPRISE LEADERSHIP

In today's fast-paced business environment, agility is no longer a luxury, it is a necessity. Enterprise leaders who master agility can navigate uncertainty, drive innovation, and sustain competitive advantage in an era of constant change. Agility in leadership is about more than just quick decision-making; it involves fostering a culture of adaptability, empowering teams, and embracing change as a driver of growth.

1. Agility as the Cornerstone of Modern Leadership

The traditional leadership model—based on rigid structures, long-term planning, and hierarchical decision-making—is rapidly becoming obsolete. In an age where market conditions shift overnight, leaders must be flexible, responsive, and proactive. Agility allows leaders to pivot, when necessary, seize new opportunities, and respond effectively to unexpected disruptions.

   i. The shift from command-and-control leadership to collaborative decision-making

   ii. Why speed and adaptability are essential for staying competitive

iii. Examples of agile leadership in action: Companies that successfully pivoted in response to market disruptions

iv. The role of decentralization in accelerating decision-making

2. Creating an Agile Organization

Enterprise agility does not rest solely on the shoulders of top executives; it must be embedded within the organization's culture, processes, and operations. Leaders must cultivate an environment where teams are empowered to experiment, innovate, and make data-driven decisions.

i. How to build a culture of agility: Encouraging flexibility, innovation, and cross-functional collaboration

ii. The importance of real-time data in agile decision-making

iii. Structuring teams for rapid execution and iterative improvements

iv. Overcoming resistance to change: Addressing fear and inertia within organizations

3. The Role of Adaptive Strategy in Leadership

A rigid, long-term strategy is no longer sufficient in an unpredictable world. Instead, leaders must embrace adaptive strategy—one that evolves based on real-time insights, shifting market dynamics, and emerging opportunities.

i. Balancing long-term vision with short-term adaptability

ii. Using scenario planning to anticipate different future outcomes

iii. Leveraging technology to enhance strategic agility (AI-driven forecasting, real-time analytics)

iv. Learning from failures: How agile organizations use setbacks to improve and iterate

4. Leading Through Disruption with Confidence

Great leaders excel in times of crisis and disruption. Instead of being paralyzed by uncertainty, agile leaders turn disruptions into opportunities by staying ahead of change, fostering resilience, and guiding teams with clarity and confidence.

i. How to remain decisive and composed in volatile markets

ii. Building resilience within teams to handle uncertainty and pressure

iii. Case studies of leaders who successfully navigated crises through agility

iv. Practical steps to future-proof leadership in a rapidly evolving business world

Agility in leadership is not just about speed, it's about adaptability, foresight, and resilience. In a world where change is the only constant, the most successful leaders are those who embrace uncertainty, empower their teams, and continuously evolve their strategies. By mastering agility, today's leaders can shape the future rather than react to it.

What Agile Leadership Looks Like in Today's Business World

Agile leadership has become a cornerstone of modern business success, enabling organizations to navigate uncertainty, drive innovation, and respond swiftly to market shifts. Unlike traditional leadership models that rely on rigid hierarchies and long-term, fixed strategies, agile leadership embraces adaptability, collaboration, and continuous learning.

Embracing a Growth Mindset

Agile leaders recognize that change is constant, and that success depends on a willingness to evolve. They foster a culture of experimentation, where failure is seen as a learning opportunity rather than a setback. This mindset encourages teams to test new ideas, iterate quickly, and refine strategies based on real-time feedback.

Decentralized Decision-Making

In an agile organization, leadership is not confined to a single executive or management tier. Instead, decision-making is distributed, empowering teams to take ownership of their projects and make informed choices. This reduces bottlenecks, increases responsiveness, and ensures that critical decisions are made by those closest to the work.

Customer Centricity and Rapid Adaptation

Modern agile leaders prioritize customer needs and market demands over internal bureaucracy. They ensure that teams remain focused on delivering value by continuously aligning business goals with customer expectations. This requires staying attuned to industry trends, leveraging data-driven insights, and being willing to pivot when necessary.

Leading Through Uncertainty

Perhaps the most defining trait of agile leadership is the ability to lead confidently in the face of uncertainty. Rather than striving for absolute control, agile leaders create an environment where teams feel safe to innovate, challenge assumptions, and adapt their strategies in real time. They cultivate resilience, ensuring that their organizations are prepared for disruption and positioned for long-term success.

By mastering agile leadership, business and enterprise professionals can navigate change with confidence, fostering a culture of adaptability and continuous improvement that drives sustainable growth.

Building an Agile Organization: Principles and Best Practices

An agile organization is not simply one that reacts quickly to change, it is a business designed for continuous evolution. Agility is embedded in its structure, culture, and strategic approach, allowing it to pivot, innovate, and stay competitive in uncertain environments. To build an agile organization, leaders must establish guiding principles and implement best practices that foster adaptability, collaboration, and resilience.

1. The Core Principles of Organizational Agility

To create an agile organization, leaders must embrace key principles that drive adaptability and innovation:

i. Customer-Centricity: Agile businesses prioritize customer needs and respond swiftly to market changes. They use data-driven insights to align products, services, and strategies with evolving customer expectations.

ii. Decentralized Decision-Making: Agility thrives when teams have the autonomy to make informed decisions quickly, without waiting for top-down directives.

iii. Iterative Execution: Instead of relying on rigid long-term plans, agile organizations use an iterative approach—testing, learning, and refining strategies based on real-world feedback.

iv. Resilience Over Predictability: Traditional organizations aim for stability and predictability, while agile organizations prioritize flexibility and resilience in the face of disruption.

2. Creating an Agile Structure: Breaking Down Silos

One of the biggest barriers to agility is organizational silos, where departments operate in isolation, hindering collaboration and innovation. Agile organizations break down these silos by:

i. Encouraging Cross-Functional Teams: Teams composed of members from different departments bring diverse perspectives and drive faster problem-solving.

ii. Implementing Agile Frameworks: Methods like Scrum, Kanban, and Lean promote iterative work cycles, continuous feedback, and rapid execution.

iii. Leveraging Digital Collaboration Tools: Cloud-based platforms, real-time dashboards, and AI-powered analytics enhance communication and efficiency across the organization.

3. Leadership's Role in Driving Agility

Agility starts at the top. Leaders must:

i. Champion a Growth Mindset: Encourage employees to embrace challenges, experiment, and view failures as learning opportunities.

ii. Empower Decision-Making at All Levels: Trusting employees to make critical decisions fosters innovation and responsiveness.

iii. Encourage Open Communication: Transparent leadership creates an environment where employees feel confident in voicing new ideas and concerns.

4. Scaling Agility Across the Organization

Once agility is established in teams, it must be scaled enterprise wide. This involves:

i. Aligning Business Strategy with Agility: Ensuring agility is not just a buzzword but a core part of the company's mission and long-term strategy.

ii. Investing in Continuous Learning: Agile organizations support ongoing education, skill-building, and knowledge-sharing to keep pace with change.

iii. Measuring Agility's Impact: Organizations should track agility through key performance indicators (KPIs), such as speed of innovation, customer satisfaction, and time-to-market for new products.

Resilience Under Pressure: Leading Through Disruptions

In today's business world, disruption is not an anomaly—it's a constant. Whether it's economic downturns, technological shifts, supply chain disruptions, or unforeseen crises, leaders must navigate uncertainty with confidence and agility. Resilience under pressure is no longer just a leadership trait; it's a critical business strategy that determines whether an organization thrives or falters.

Staying Calm Amid Uncertainty

The best leaders remain composed when faced with volatility. Panic-driven decisions can amplify challenges, whereas a steady and rational approach helps teams stay focused and proactive.

Resilient leaders cultivate emotional intelligence, balancing urgency with thoughtful decision-making to maintain stability.

Adapting Speed and Precision

Resilience is not about resisting change—it's about adapting to it effectively. Businesses that survive disruptions are those that pivot quickly, realign priorities, and take decisive action. This requires a mindset that embraces flexibility, continuous learning, and scenario planning to prepare for multiple potential outcomes.

Strengthening Organizational Agility

A resilient organization doesn't just rely on strong leadership; it builds agility into its core structure. Companies that empower teams to make informed decisions, experiment with new approaches, and leverage technology to stay ahead are more likely to withstand disruptions. Leaders must foster a culture where adaptability is encouraged at every level of the business.

Turning Crisis into Opportunity

Every disruption presents an opportunity for reinvention. Resilient leaders use challenges as a catalyst for innovation, re-evaluating business models, processes, and market strategies. By viewing setbacks as a chance to evolve, organizations can emerge stronger and more competitive in the long run.

Mastering change in the face of disruptions requires more than just endurance, demands proactive leadership, strategic adaptability, and an unwavering commitment to long-term growth. The ability to lead through uncertainty is what separates resilient businesses from those that struggle to recover.

From Strategy to Execution: Embedding Agility in Business Operations

Agility is not just a leadership philosophy—it must be embedded into the operational fabric of an organization. Enterprises that successfully integrate agility into their strategies, structures, and processes can quickly pivot in response to market shifts, technological advancements, and evolving customer demands.

a. Aligning Strategy with Real-Time Adaptation

Traditional business strategies often rely on rigid long-term plans that assume stable market conditions. However, in an era of rapid disruption, static strategies become obsolete quickly. Agile enterprises embrace dynamic planning, where strategies are continuously assessed and refined based on real-time data, competitive intelligence, and emerging trends. This shift from rigid planning to adaptive execution enables organizations to remain responsive and proactive rather than reactive.

b. Operational Flexibility: Creating Systems That Can Pivot

Embedding agility into business operations requires designing systems, workflows, and supply chains that can quickly adapt to changing conditions. This includes leveraging cloud-based infrastructure for scalability, implementing modular product development approaches, and ensuring cross-functional teams can collaborate seamlessly. Organizations that build flexibility into their operations gain a competitive edge by being able to seize opportunities and mitigate risks faster than their competitors.

c. Leveraging Agile Methodologies for Execution

Many leading enterprises adopt agile methodologies—borrowed from software development—to enhance adaptability across business functions. Frameworks such as Scrum, Lean, and Kanban emphasize iterative execution, cross-functional collaboration, and continuous feedback loops. By applying agile methodologies to everything from product development to marketing and finance, organizations can accelerate execution, minimize inefficiencies, and drive innovation at scale.

d. Measuring and Refining Agility in Business Performance

To ensure agility is truly embedded in business operations, organizations must establish key performance indicators (KPIs) that track adaptability, responsiveness, and innovation. Metrics such as time-to-market, speed of decision-making, and employee engagement in change initiatives help leaders gauge their organization's agility. Continuous monitoring and refinement of these indicators ensure that agility remains a sustained competitive advantage rather than a one-time initiative.

By translating agility from a strategic vision into tangible execution, enterprises position themselves to thrive in a constantly evolving market. Leaders who champion operational agility create resilient organizations that are not only prepared for change but actively shape the future of their industries.

CHAPTER FOUR
LIFELONG LEARNING IN A COMPETITIVE BUSINESS ENVIRONMENT

In an era of rapid technological advancements and shifting market demands, the most successful professionals and organizations are those that embrace continuous learning. Lifelong learning is no longer an option, it is a strategic imperative for staying relevant, competitive, and innovative. Businesses that foster a culture of learning gain a sustainable advantage, while individuals who commit to continuous skill development position themselves as leaders in their industries.

1. The Strategic Importance of Lifelong Learning

Lifelong learning is not just about acquiring new knowledge—it's about developing the mindset and habits that enable professionals to adapt, innovate, and lead in an ever-changing business environment. Organizations that invest in learning and development (L&D) outperform those that resist change.

Key reasons why lifelong learning is essential for business success:

> **i. Keeping Pace with Emerging Technologies:** AI, automation, and digital transformation are reshaping industries. Continuous

learning helps professionals and enterprises stay ahead of the curve.

ii. Enhancing Adaptability and Problem-Solving: In a volatile market, the ability to learn and apply new skills quickly is a critical asset.

iii. Fostering Innovation and Creativity: Exposure to new ideas, trends, and methodologies fuels innovation and allows businesses to anticipate shifts before they happen.

iv. Attracting and Retaining Top Talent: Employees are more engaged and loyal to companies that invest in their professional development.

2. Building a Learning Culture in the Enterprise

For lifelong learning to thrive, businesses must create an environment that encourages and rewards continuous skill development. A strong learning culture fosters resilience, collaboration, and agility across the organization.

Key Strategies for Building a Learning Culture:

i. Encouraging Curiosity and Experimentation: Organizations should support employees in exploring new skills, taking calculated risks, and learning from failures.

ii. Embedding Learning in Daily Workflows: Instead of limiting learning to formal training programs, businesses can integrate micro learning, mentorship, and hands-on projects into daily operations.

iii. Leveraging Technology for Scalable Learning: AI-powered learning platforms, virtual training sessions, and personalized development plans make learning accessible and scalable.

iv. Recognizing and Rewarding Learning Achievements: Encouraging employees to pursue certifications, attend industry conferences, and contribute to knowledge-sharing, strengthens a company's learning culture.

3. The Evolving Skill Set for Future Business Leaders

As industries transform, so do the skills required to lead effectively. Professionals who embrace lifelong learning must focus on both technical and soft skills to remain valuable.

Essential Skills for Future Business Leaders:

I. Digital Literacy: Understanding AI, data analytics, and digital transformation is crucial for making informed strategic decisions.

ii. Adaptability and Agility: The ability to pivot and respond to change is a defining characteristic of high-performing leaders.

iii. Critical Thinking and Problem-Solving: In a world of information overload, the ability to analyze, synthesize, and apply knowledge is more valuable than ever.

iv. Collaboration and Emotional Intelligence (EQ): Strong interpersonal skills enable leaders to build high-performing teams and drive meaningful change.

v. Continuous Reinvention: Leaders must develop the habit of regularly updating their skills and knowledge base to stay relevant.

4. Implementing Lifelong Learning for Business Growth

To truly master change, businesses must shift from viewing learning as a one-time event to embedding it into their long-term strategy.

Best Practices for Implementing Lifelong Learning:

i. Develop Personalized Learning Pathways: Employees should have access to tailored learning experiences that align with their roles and career goals.

ii. Encourage Cross-Disciplinary Learning: Exposure to different fields and industries sparks innovation and broadens problem-solving capabilities.

iii. Invest in Leadership Development: Future-proofing an organization requires continuous investment in leadership training and mentorship programs.

iv. Measure Learning Impact on Business Performance: Tracking employee growth, productivity gains, and innovation metrics ensures learning initiatives deliver tangible results.

Lifelong Learning as a Competitive Advantage

In a business landscape defined by disruption, learning is the single most powerful tool for mastering change. Organizations that prioritize lifelong learning build adaptable, resilient workforces ready to tackle tomorrow's challenges. Similarly, professionals who embrace continuous skill development ensure they remain indispensable in an evolving marketplace.

By embedding learning into the fabric of corporate strategy, businesses and leaders don't just keep up with change, they drive it.

The Evolution of Skills in a Rapidly Changing Economy

The modern business landscape is defined by rapid technological advancements, shifting market demands, and unpredictable global events. Traditional skills that once ensured job security are now evolving or becoming obsolete at an unprecedented rate. For business and enterprise professionals, mastering change means continuously developing new capabilities, embracing adaptability, and preparing for the future of work.

From Specialized Expertise to Hybrid Skills

Gone are the days when deep specialization in a single domain was enough to ensure career longevity. Today, professionals must cultivate hybrid skills—a blend of technical proficiency, strategic thinking, and soft skills like communication and leadership. The most valuable employees and leaders are those who can bridge multiple disciplines, combining analytical abilities with creativity, emotional intelligence, and adaptability.

Digital Fluency as a Non-Negotiable

As automation, AI, and data-driven decision-making become central to business operations, digital literacy is no longer optional. Professionals who understand how to leverage technology to improve efficiency and drive strategic growth will have a distinct advantage. This doesn't mean everyone must become a coder or data scientist, but familiarity with digital tools, platforms, and analytics is crucial for making informed decisions in a tech-driven environment.

The Rise of Continuous Learning

In the past, formal education was often seen as the primary pathway to career success. However, in a rapidly changing economy, the ability to learn, unlearn, and relearn has become more critical than any single degree or certification. Organizations are increasingly valuing employees who take ownership of their professional development—whether through online courses, industry certifications, or hands-on experience in evolving fields.

Soft Skills as a Competitive Advantage

While technical expertise remains important, soft skills like adaptability, critical thinking, collaboration, and emotional intelligence are becoming the true differentiators in leadership and business success. The ability to navigate uncertainty, manage diverse teams, and communicate effectively in high-pressure situations is what allows professionals to thrive amid change.

Mastering Change in the Skills Economy

For business leaders and professionals, the ability to anticipate and respond to skill shifts is crucial. Those who cultivate agility, invest in lifelong learning, and embrace new ways of thinking will not only survive change but use it as a steppingstone for innovation and growth. The future belongs to those who are willing to evolve with it.

Building a Culture of Curiosity and Continuous Improvement

In an era of relentless change, organizations that cultivate a culture of curiosity and continuous improvement remain ahead of the competition. Enterprise leaders who foster an environment where employees question the status quo, seek better solutions, and embrace learning create businesses that are more innovative, resilient, and adaptable to disruption.

a. Encouraging a Growth Mindset at Every Level

A culture of curiosity begins with a growth mindset—the belief that abilities, skills, and intelligence can be developed through effort and learning. Leaders must actively promote this mindset by encouraging employees to take on challenges, experiment with new ideas, and view failures as opportunities for growth. When continuous learning is embedded into an organization's DNA, employees become more willing to explore innovative approaches and embrace change.

b. Creating Safe Spaces for Experimentation

Fear of failure stifles innovation. Businesses that lead in times of uncertainty build environments where employees feel safe to test new ideas, challenge existing processes, and take calculated risks. By establishing innovation labs, hackathons, and cross-functional brainstorming sessions, organizations can encourage employees to think creatively without the fear of negative repercussions. A culture that rewards experimentation fosters continuous improvement and breakthrough innovations.

c. Implementing Systems for Ongoing Learning and Development

Continuous improvement requires structured learning opportunities. Organizations that invest in upskilling and reskilling programs—through mentorship, online courses, certifications, and hands-on training—empower employees to stay relevant in an ever-changing business landscape. Additionally, businesses that integrate knowledge-sharing platforms and peer-learning networks ensure that employees can easily access and contribute to collective expertise.

d. Embedding Feedback Loops for Continuous Refinement

A culture of continuous improvement thrives on feedback. Organizations that implement regular feedback loops—both internally and externally—gain insights into what works and what needs adjustment. Employee feedback mechanisms, customer insights, and performance analytics provide the necessary data to refine strategies, optimize processes, and enhance innovation. By making feedback an integral part of decision-making, companies can adapt more quickly to market changes and internal challenges.

By building a culture that values curiosity, learning, and iteration, enterprises can transform change from a disruptive force into a source of continuous growth. Leaders who cultivate this mindset within their organizations will not only future-proof their business but also create an environment where innovation flourishes and success is sustained.

Upskilling and Reskilling: Staying Relevant in a Shifting Job Market

The rapid pace of technological advancements, automation, and evolving market dynamics are reshaping the job landscape at an unprecedented rate. As industries undergo digital transformation, many traditional roles are being disrupted, while new opportunities emerge. To remain competitive, professionals and businesses must prioritize upskilling—enhancing existing skills—and reskilling—learning entirely new competencies to transition into different roles.

For business leaders, mastering change means fostering a culture where employees continuously develop new skills that align with future demands. Organizations that fail to invest in workforce development risk stagnation, skill gaps, and loss of competitive advantage.

1. The Urgency of Upskilling and Reskilling in Today's Market

In a world where automation and AI are reshaping job roles, learning agility has become a critical differentiator. A World Economic Forum report predicts that nearly half of today's workforce will need reskilling within the next few years due to technological disruption.

Key drivers behind the need for upskilling and reskilling include:

> **i. AI and Automation:** Routine tasks are being automated, requiring professionals to develop skills in emerging technologies, data analysis, and strategic decision-making.

> **ii. Industry Convergence:** Sectors such as finance, healthcare, and retail are integrating digital tools, necessitating interdisciplinary knowledge.

> **iii. The Shift to Remote and Hybrid Work:** Digital collaboration, cybersecurity, and virtual communication skills have become essential.

> **iv. Evolving Customer Expectations:** Businesses must continuously adapt to changing consumer behaviors, requiring agile marketing, data-driven insights, and personalized customer engagement strategies.

Companies that proactively train their workforce are better positioned to innovate, retain talent, and maintain a competitive edge.

2. Identifying the Right Skills for the Future

To master change, businesses and professionals must anticipate the skills that will drive success in the coming years.

Key Areas for Upskilling and Reskilling:

   i. Digital and Data Literacy: Understanding how to interpret data, leverage AI, and applying analytics is becoming a baseline skill in almost every industry.

   ii. Agile Thinking and Problem-Solving: The ability to navigate complexity, adapt quickly, and apply critical thinking is highly valued in uncertain markets.

   iii. Technical Skills in Emerging Technologies: AI, machine learning, cloud computing, and blockchain are transforming industries, making expertise in these areas increasingly essential.

   iv. Soft Skills and Leadership Abilities: Emotional intelligence, collaboration, and change management are critical for leading teams in a fast-changing environment.

   v. Cybersecurity and Privacy Awareness: As digital transformation accelerates, protecting data and ensuring compliance with regulations is more important than ever.

3. Implementing Upskilling and Reskilling Strategies in the Enterprise

For businesses, workforce transformation is not just about hiring new talent—it's about enabling existing employees to evolve alongside the organization. Effective upskilling and reskilling strategies ensure that companies remain agile and competitive while reducing turnover and talent shortages.

Steps to Implement a Successful Learning Initiative:

i. Conduct a Skills Gap Analysis: Identify the capabilities employees need to develop to meet future business objectives.

ii. Leverage AI-Powered Learning Platforms: Use adaptive learning technologies that personalize training experiences for each employee.

iii. Encourage a Learning Mindset: Reward employees for acquiring new skills and creating internal mobility opportunities.

iv. Provide On-the-Job Learning Opportunities: Blended learning—combining formal courses with hands-on experience—enhances skill retention and application.

v. Develop Leadership in Learning: Executives and managers should lead, by example, continuously learning and mentoring their teams.

Organizations that prioritize upskilling and reskilling not only prove future proof their workforce but also strengthen their ability to navigate disruption and seize new opportunities.

4. The Role of Businesses and Individuals in Lifelong Learning

Both companies and professionals share responsibility in ensuring continuous learning remains a priority.

For Businesses:

i. Create an ecosystem where learning is embedded in daily workflows.

ii. Foster collaboration between HR, L&D, and leadership teams to align learning with business goals.

iii. Develop partnerships with universities, online platforms, and industry experts to facilitate continuous education.

For Individuals:

i. Take ownership of personal development by seeking out courses, certifications, and industry events.

ii. Cultivate a growth mindset—viewing new challenges as learning opportunities rather than obstacles.

iii. Stay updated on industry trends and proactively acquire skills that will be in high demand.

Future-Proofing Careers and Organizations

In a constantly evolving job market, upskilling and reskilling are no longer optional; they are essential for survival and success. Businesses that invest in continuous learning create agile, future-ready workforces, while professionals who embrace lifelong learning unlock new career opportunities and remain indispensable in their industries.

Mastering change in today's business environment requires adaptability, curiosity, and a commitment to growth—qualities that define the leaders and innovators of tomorrow.

Bridging the Gap Between Learning and Business Impact

In the fast-moving world of business and enterprise, learning is only as valuable as the results it drives. Organizations that invest in upskilling their workforce without a clear strategy for applying new knowledge risk wasting resources and falling behind competitors who integrate learning into their business objectives. To master change, businesses must bridge the gap between continuous learning and real-world impact, ensuring that education translates into measurable performance improvements and innovation.

Aligning Learning with Strategic Goals

To drive real business impact, learning initiatives must be directly tied to the company's strategic objectives. Whether the goal is to improve operational efficiency, enhance customer experience, or expand into new markets, training programs should be designed to equip employees with the specific skills needed to achieve these outcomes. A disconnect between corporate learning and business priorities results in wasted potential, as employees may gain knowledge that doesn't align with the company's evolving needs.

Implementing Learning in Real-Time

Many organizations struggle to turn theoretical knowledge into practical application. Learning should not be confined to classrooms or online courses but embedded into daily workflows. Companies that integrate real-time learning—through job rotations, mentorship, on-the-job coaching, and real-world problem-solving—ensure that employees immediately apply new skills in meaningful ways. This hands-on approach accelerates the learning curve and leads to tangible improvements in business performance.

Measuring the ROI of Learning Initiatives

To ensure learning translates into impact, businesses must track its return on investment (ROI). This means moving beyond participation metrics and evaluating how training influences productivity, innovation, customer satisfaction, and profitability. Key performance indicators (KPIs) should be established to measure how newly acquired skills drive business outcomes, such as increased revenue, improved decision-making, or enhanced operational efficiency. Data-driven insights help organizations refine learning programs for maximum effectiveness.

Creating a Culture of Business-Driven Learning

For learning to make a lasting impact, it must become part of the organization's culture. Leaders play a crucial role in modeling continuous learning and demonstrating how it contributes to business success. Encouraging employees to take ownership of their professional development, while providing opportunities to apply their knowledge in meaningful projects, fosters a workforce that is both skilled and business minded.

By intentionally linking learning to business impact, organizations can ensure that education isn't just an expense but a driver of growth, resilience, and competitive advantage. In a world of constant change, the ability to continuously learn and immediately apply new knowledge will determine which businesses thrive and which are left behind.

CHAPTER FIVE
THE BUSINESS IMPACT OF EMERGING TECHNOLOGIES AND MARKET SHIFTS

Technology and market dynamics are evolving at an unprecedented rate, reshaping industries, disrupting traditional business models, and creating new opportunities. From artificial intelligence and blockchain to the rise of decentralized finance and digital-first consumer behaviors, companies must continuously adapt to stay competitive.

For business and enterprise professionals, mastering change means understanding how emerging technologies drive transformation, identifying potential market shifts before they happen, and strategically leveraging innovation to gain a competitive edge.

1. Emerging Technologies Reshaping Business

Technological advancements are no longer optional; they are fundamental to survival and growth. Businesses that fail to adopt emerging technologies risk obsolescence, while those that integrate them strategically can unlock new efficiencies, revenue streams, and competitive advantages.

Key Technologies Impacting Business Today

   i. Artificial Intelligence (AI) and Machine Learning (ML): Automating decision-making, personalizing customer experiences, and optimizing operations.

   ii. Blockchain and Decentralized Finance (DeFi): Transforming transactions, contracts, and supply chain transparency.

   iii. Cloud Computing and Edge Computing: Enabling scalability, security, and real-time data access.

   iv. 5G and IoT (Internet of Things): Connecting devices, improving automation, and enhancing operational intelligence.

   v. Quantum Computing: Revolutionizing data processing power and security.

Forward-thinking businesses actively explore these innovations, integrating them into their strategies to enhance efficiency, reduce costs, and drive growth.

2. Market Shifts Driving Business Transformation

Technological disruption goes hand in hand with shifts in consumer behavior, regulatory environments, and economic landscapes. Understanding these trends is essential for mastering change in business.

Key Market Trends Reshaping Industries

i. The Digital-First Economy: Customers expect seamless online experiences, from e-commerce to virtual services.

ii. Workforce Transformation: Remote work, hybrid models, and gig economy trends are redefining talent management.

iii. Sustainability and ESG (Environmental, Social, Governance): Businesses are being held accountable for ethical and sustainable practices.

iv. Regulatory Changes: Data privacy laws, AI ethics regulations, and compliance requirements are shaping operational strategies.

v. Shifting Global Supply Chains: Trade disruptions, geopolitical tensions, and resource shortages demand more resilient logistics and procurement strategies.

Businesses that track these trends can proactively adapt rather than react, positioning themselves ahead of competitors.

3. Adapting to Disruption: Strategies for Enterprises

Thriving in an era of disruption requires more than just adopting technology, it requires a culture of agility and innovation.

Strategic Approaches to Adapting

i. Agile Business Models: Companies must be flexible, able to pivot quickly in response to changes in the market.

ii. Continuous Innovation: Investing in R&D and fostering an experimentation mindset keeps businesses ahead of the curve.

iii. Data-Driven Decision-Making: Leveraging AI, big data, and predictive analytics ensures more informed strategic moves.

iv. Customer-Centric Adaptation: Businesses must align with shifting consumer demands, personalizing products and services accordingly.

v. Ecosystem Partnerships: Collaborating with startups, tech firms, and research institutions accelerates innovation.

Companies that master these strategies turn disruption into a competitive advantage rather than a risk.

4. The Future of Business: Preparing for the Next Wave of Change

As technology and market forces continue to evolve, businesses must remain future-focused.

How to Future-Proof an organization

i. Invest in Digital Transformation: Companies that fully embrace digital tools and automation will remain resilient.

ii. Cultivate a Culture of Lifelong Learning: Workforce adaptability is key to sustaining competitive advantage.

iii. Monitor and Predict Industry Trends: Leaders should leverage market intelligence and scenario planning to stay ahead.

Embrace Ethical Innovation: Trust and transparency will be critical differentiators in the business landscape.

iv. Be Ready for Industry Convergence: Boundaries between industries are blurring companies and must be open to reinventing their business models.

The business world will continue to experience rapid shifts, but enterprises that anticipate, adapt, and innovate will not just survive, they will lead.

By mastering change, business and enterprise professionals can harness the power of emerging technologies and market shifts to drive sustained success in an increasingly unpredictable world.

How Disruptive Technologies Are Reshaping Industries

In today's fast-paced business environment, disruptive technologies are redefining entire industries, altering business models, and shifting competitive landscapes. Organizations that embrace these innovations gain a strategic edge, while those that resist change risk becoming obsolete. From artificial intelligence and automation to blockchain and quantum computing, technological advancements are not just improving efficiency, they are rewriting the rules of engagement in every sector.

Businesses must recognize that disruption is no longer an occasional event but an ongoing reality. Companies like Uber transformed transportation, Netflix revolutionized entertainment, and Amazon redefined retail. These shifts happened because organizations leveraged technology to meet evolving consumer demands faster and more effectively than their competitors. The key takeaway for business leaders is that innovation does not wait—companies must continuously adapt or risk irrelevance.

One of the biggest challenges for enterprises is integrating new technologies without disrupting their core operations. Adopting AI-driven analytics, for example, can significantly enhance decision-making, but it requires a shift in mindset and investment in talent development. Similarly, blockchain is transforming supply chain transparency, but businesses must rethink how they manage data security and transactions. Leaders must strike a balance between innovation and operational stability, ensuring that technological transformation aligns with business goals.

The impact of disruptive technologies extends beyond businesses to the workforce itself. Automation and AI are redefining roles, requiring professionals to upskill and adapt. Jobs that were once manual are now being handled by intelligent systems, and employees must focus on higher-value tasks such as strategic thinking and problem-solving. Companies that invest in continuous learning and digital transformation will be the ones that not only survive but thrive in this new era.

Ultimately, mastering change in the face of technological disruption means fostering a culture of adaptability. Businesses that encourage experimentation, embrace emerging trends, and remain open to reinvention will lead the industries of the future. Those that fail to do so will watch as more agile competitors take their place.

The Intersection of Market Trends and Technological Advancements

In today's business landscape, staying ahead requires more than just reacting to market shifts—it demands a proactive approach to integrating emerging technologies with evolving industry trends. Companies that master change understand that technology is not just a tool but a strategic enabler, shaping how businesses operate, compete, and deliver value. The convergence of market trends and technological advancements creates new opportunities and challenges, requiring business leaders to navigate this intersection with agility and foresight.

How Market Trends Shape Technological Adoption

Market demands influence the pace at which businesses adopt new technologies. Consumer expectations for speed, personalization, and convenience drive companies to implement AI, automation, and data analytics. Economic fluctuations push businesses toward cost-efficient digital solutions, while regulatory changes necessitate advanced compliance technologies. Companies that closely monitor market signals can align their tech investments with real-world needs, ensuring they remain competitive in dynamic environments.

Technology as a Disruptor and Enabler

Emerging technologies can disrupt entire industries, forcing businesses to either adapt or risk obsolescence. The rise of e-commerce reshaped retail, cloud computing transformed IT infrastructure, and AI-driven analytics revolutionized decision-making. Yet, technology is also an enabler—businesses that leverage digital tools effectively can optimize operations, unlock new revenue streams, and enhance customer experiences. Mastering change means recognizing when technology is a threat and when it is an opportunity for reinvention.

Balancing Innovation with Business Viability

Not all technological advancements align with business goals, and chasing every new trend can lead to wasted resources. Successful enterprises balance innovation with strategic execution, adopting technologies that drive efficiency, scalability, and long-term growth. Leaders must evaluate emerging tools through the lens of business impact—whether improving internal processes, enhancing customer engagement, or creating new market opportunities.

Building a Future-Ready Business

To thrive at the intersection of market trends and technology, companies must foster a culture of adaptability. This means continuously assessing industry changes, investing in digital capabilities, and ensuring teams have the skills to leverage new tools effectively. Businesses that embrace change as an ongoing process, rather than a one-time adjustment, position themselves as industry leaders, ready to evolve alongside shifting market dynamics.

By mastering this intersection, businesses can turn uncertainty into opportunity, using technology not just to respond to trends but to shape them.

Balancing Innovation and Risk in Tech-Driven Business Models

In a rapidly evolving business landscape, innovation is essential for growth, differentiation, and long-term success. However, innovation also comes with inherent risks—ranging from operational disruptions to regulatory challenges and market unpredictability. Business leaders must strike the right balance between embracing technological advancements and managing the risks associated with rapid change.

Mastering this balance requires a structured approach that ensures innovation drives sustainable business value while mitigating potential downsides. Companies that navigate this challenge successfully position themselves as market leaders, while those that ignore risk management can face costly failures.

1. Understanding the Dual Nature of Innovation

Innovation can be a double-edged sword—when implemented effectively, it creates a competitive advantage; when mismanaged, it leads to inefficiencies, financial losses, and reputational damage.

Key Opportunities of Innovation

i. Market Leadership: Early adoption of new technologies allows businesses to set industry standards.

ii. Operational Efficiency: Automation, AI, and data analytics improve productivity and decision-making.

iii. Enhanced Customer Experience: Digital transformation enables personalization and seamless interactions.

iv. Revenue Growth: New products, services, and business models unlock untapped market potential.

Common Risks of Innovation

i. Financial Exposure: R&D and technology investments can be costly and uncertain.

ii. Regulatory and Compliance Issues: Emerging technologies often lack clear legal frameworks, posing risks.

iii. Cybersecurity Threats: Digital innovation increases vulnerability to data breaches and cyberattacks.

iv. Market Resistance: Customers and stakeholders may be slow to adopt new innovations.

Business leaders must acknowledge these risks while ensuring they do not become barriers to progress.

2. Implementing a Risk-Aware Innovation Strategy

For businesses to thrive in a tech-driven economy, innovation must be intentional, strategic, and aligned with risk management frameworks.

Strategies for Balancing Innovation and Risk

i. Agile Experimentation: Deploy small-scale pilots before full-scale implementation to assess viability.

ii. Cross-Functional Collaboration: Involve legal, compliance, IT, and business units in innovation strategies.

iii. Scenario Planning: Assess potential risks and develop mitigation strategies before scaling innovations.

iv. Customer-Centric Development: Validate new solutions with end-users to ensure market fitness and adoption.

v. Fail-Fast, Learn-Fast Approach: Encourage iterative improvements rather than waiting for perfection.

A structured yet flexible approach ensures businesses can innovate while minimizing exposure to unforeseen challenges.

3. Managing Regulatory, Ethical, and Security Concerns

The rapid pace of technological advancement often outstrips regulatory and ethical frameworks, creating legal uncertainties and reputational risks.

Regulatory and Ethical Considerations

i. Data Privacy Compliance: Adhering to laws like GDPR, CCPA, and industry-specific regulations.

ii. AI and Bias Mitigation: Ensuring fairness, transparency, and accountability in AI-driven decision-making.

iii. Sustainability and ESG Factors: Innovating responsibly with environmental and social considerations in mind.

iv. Security by Design: Embedding cybersecurity measures into digital products and services from the outset.

A proactive approach to these concerns not only prevents regulatory issues but also builds trust with customers and stakeholders.

4. Turning Risk Management into a Competitive Advantage

The most successful businesses do not just mitigate risks, they leverage them as a source of competitive advantage.

How to Innovate with Confidence

i. Develop a Risk-Resilient Culture: Encourage teams to take calculated risks while remaining accountable.

ii. Invest in Governance and Compliance Technology: Use AI and automation to monitor compliance in real time.

iii. Monitor Market Trends and Competitor Moves: Stay ahead of regulatory changes and industry shifts.

iv. Educate and Train Teams on Risk Awareness: Ensure employees understand the risks associated with innovation.

v. Leverage Strategic Partnerships: Collaborate with industry leaders, regulators, and tech experts to co-create solutions.

When businesses integrate risk intelligence into their innovation strategies, they build resilience, enhance credibility, and maintain a sustainable path to growth.

Mastering change in a technology-driven business landscape requires both bold innovation and smart risk management. Companies that successfully balance the two will not only navigate uncertainty effectively but will emerge as industry pioneers.

Case Studies: Businesses That Thrived (or Failed) Due to Market Shifts

In an era defined by rapid technological advancements, shifting consumer behaviors, and economic uncertainty, businesses must be prepared to evolve—or risk obsolescence. The ability to anticipate change, pivot strategies, and leverage innovation has separated thriving enterprises from those that failed to adapt. Below, we examine notable case studies of businesses that successfully navigated market disruptions, as well as those that struggled to keep pace.

Thriving Businesses: Embracing Change and Innovation

Netflix: From DVD Rentals to Streaming Giant

Netflix's transition from a DVD rental service to a global streaming powerhouse exemplifies strategic adaptability. Recognizing the shift in consumer preferences and the potential of digital content delivery, Netflix pivoted its business model in the mid-2000s. By investing in technology, original content, and data-driven personalization, the company not only survived the decline of physical media but redefined the entertainment industry.

Key Takeaway: Companies that continuously anticipate consumer needs and invest in innovation can turn industry disruptions into opportunities.

Microsoft: Reinventing Itself in the Cloud Era

Once seen as a legacy software company, Microsoft successfully transformed itself by embracing cloud computing under CEO Satya Nadella's leadership. The company's aggressive push into enterprise cloud solutions with Azure helped it regain relevance and become a leader in cloud services, competing with Amazon Web Services (AWS). This strategic shift propelled Microsoft to new heights, reinforcing the power of reinvention in the face of market evolution.

Key Takeaway: Businesses must be willing to shift their core focus to align with emerging technological trends and customer demands.

Domino's Pizza: Winning with Digital Transformation

In the early 2000s, Domino's was struggling with declining sales and customer dissatisfaction. Instead of merely tweaking its menu, the company embraced digital transformation. It revamped its online ordering system, launched a mobile app, and invested in data analytics to improve customer experience and delivery efficiency. This shift paid off, making Domino's a tech-driven pizza leader and significantly increasing its market share.

Key Takeaway: Businesses that leverage technology to enhance customer experience can gain a competitive edge even in traditional industries.

Failed Businesses: Resistance to Change and Market Realities

Blockbuster: The Cost of Ignoring Digital Disruption

At its peak, Blockbuster was the dominant force in home entertainment rentals. However, its reluctance to adopt a digital-first strategy led to its downfall. The company had the opportunity to acquire Netflix early on but dismissed the digital shift, failing to recognize the growing demand for online streaming. As a result, Blockbuster became obsolete, while Netflix flourished.

Key Takeaway: Businesses that fail to acknowledge and act on disruptive trends risk losing relevance.

Kodak: Innovation Without Execution

Kodak was once synonymous with photography, yet it failed to capitalize on the digital revolution. Ironically, Kodak invented the digital camera but hesitated to commercialize it, fearing it would cannibalize its film business. This hesitation allowed competitors like Canon and Sony to dominate the digital photography market, leading to Kodak's decline and bankruptcy.

Key Takeaway: Fear of disrupting one's own business model can lead to stagnation and eventual obsolescence.

Nokia: Falling Behind in the Smartphone Race

Nokia was a global leader in mobile phones but failed to adapt to the rise of smartphones and touch-screen technology. While Apple and Android manufacturers innovated rapidly, Nokia clung to its outdated Symbian OS and slow-moving product development cycles. By the time the company attempted to catch up, it was too late, and Nokia's market dominance had vanished.

Key Takeaway: Businesses must stay agile and embrace emerging technologies to remain competitive in fast-evolving industries.

Lessons for Business Leaders

These case studies reveal critical insights into mastering change in today's business landscape:

> **i. Anticipate and embrace change:** Companies must remain forward-thinking and recognize industry shifts before they become crises.
>
> **ii. Invest in innovation and digital transformation:** Technology is a catalyst for growth and leveraging it effectively can ensure long-term success.

Iii. Be willing to disrupt your own model: Fear of change can be more damaging than the change itself. Businesses that embrace transformation early gain a significant advantage.

iv. Stay customer-centric: Understanding and responding to evolving consumer needs is essential for sustained relevance.

Mastering change requires businesses to be proactive, adaptable, and willing to evolve. Those that do will thrive in an unpredictable world, while those that resist will struggle to survive.

MARIE TONGS

CHAPTER SIX
THE FUTURE OF WORK LEADING IN AN ERA OF TRANSFORMATION

The way we work is changing at an unprecedented pace. From the rapid adoption of AI and automation to the rise of remote and hybrid workplaces, business leaders must navigate a world where traditional management approaches no longer suffice. The future of work isn't just about technology, it's about how leaders can adapt to shifting employee expectations, evolving business models, and continuous market disruptions.

Redefining Leadership in a Digital-First World

Leadership in the modern era requires more than just expertise and decision-making skills. Today's leaders must be agile, empathetic, and adaptable, fostering a culture of continuous learning and innovation. The shift to digital workflows and global collaboration demands that executives move beyond hierarchical leadership and embrace more dynamic, inclusive management styles. Companies that cultivate leaders who can inspire and empower teams in a distributed, technology-driven environment will have a competitive edge in the evolving business landscape.

The Skills Revolution: Preparing for a Workforce Shift

The rapid transformation of industries means that the skills required for success are constantly evolving. While technical proficiency remains important, soft skills—such as problem-solving, adaptability, and critical thinking—are becoming equally valuable. Employees and leaders alike must prioritize lifelong learning, leveraging upskilling initiatives, mentorship programs, and real-time training to stay relevant. Organizations that invest in developing their workforce will not only retain top talent but also drive sustainable business growth.

Embracing a Hybrid and Remote Work Economy

The shift to remote and hybrid work models is no longer a temporary adjustment, it is a fundamental change in how businesses operate. Companies that embrace flexibility and autonomy while maintaining productivity and collaboration will be the ones that thrive. Leading in this new era means creating environments that foster engagement, trust, and accountability. The right mix of digital tools, clear communication strategies, and employee well-being initiatives will determine an organization's ability to succeed in a decentralized work environment.

The Role of AI and Automation in Workforce Transformation

AI and automation are reshaping job roles across industries, augmenting human capabilities rather than replacing them. Businesses that strategically integrate AI into their operations can enhance efficiency, drive data-informed decision-making, and unlock new value streams. However, with this transformation comes the responsibility to ensure that employees are empowered to work alongside intelligent systems, rather than being displaced by them. Forward-thinking leaders will focus on reskilling their workforce and aligning AI adoption with ethical considerations and human oversight.

Leading the Future with Confidence

Mastering change in the future of work means embracing transformation as a continuous process. The most successful leaders will not only adapt to new technologies and business models but will also shape them. By fostering agility, innovation, and a people-centric approach, businesses can build resilient organizations that are prepared for whatever comes next.

The Workforce of Tomorrow: What's Changing and Why?

The nature of work is evolving at an unprecedented pace, driven by technological advancements, demographic shifts, and changing employee expectations. As businesses strive to remain competitive, understanding the forces reshaping the workforce of tomorrow is critical to building resilient, adaptive organizations.

1. The Rise of Automation and AI

Automation and artificial intelligence (AI) are transforming job roles across industries. Repetitive and routine tasks are increasingly being handled by intelligent systems, freeing human workers to focus on complex problem-solving, creativity, and strategic decision-making.

    i. AI-driven chatbots and virtual assistants are handling customer service interactions.

    ii. Robotic process automation (RPA) is streamlining administrative functions.

    iii. Machine learning algorithms enhancing decision-making in finance, healthcare, and marketing.

While automation will replace certain jobs, it will also create new opportunities in AI ethics, cybersecurity, and digital transformation leadership. The key to workforce sustainability lies in upskilling employees to work alongside intelligent systems rather than being replaced by them.

2. The Shift Toward Remote and Hybrid Work

The COVID-19 pandemic accelerated the adoption of remote and hybrid work models, and this shift is proving to be more than just a temporary adjustment. Employees now expect flexibility, with many prioritizing work-life balance over traditional office structures

    i. Companies are investing in remote collaboration tools and virtual workspaces.

    ii. Hybrid work models allow employees to split time between home and office environments.

iii. The gig economy is expanding, with professionals choosing freelance or contract work over full-time employment.

Organizations that fail to embrace flexible work arrangements may struggle to attract and retain top talent in the years to come.

3. A Greater Emphasis on Skills Over Degrees

The workforce of tomorrow will prioritize skills and competencies over formal degrees. Traditional hiring practices that focus on educational qualifications are giving way to skills-based assessments, micro-credentialing, and competency-based hiring.

i. Companies like Google, Apple, and Tesla have de-emphasized degree requirements for many roles.

ii. Online learning platforms and corporate training programs are enabling lifelong learning.

iii. Employees are expected to engage in continuous upskilling to remain relevant.

Businesses that invest in skills development and career growth opportunities will build a workforce that is both agile and future ready.

4. The Growing Importance of Diversity, Equity, and Inclusion (DEI)

Diversity, equity, and inclusion (DEI) are no longer optional, they are business imperatives. A diverse workforce fosters innovation, enhances problem-solving, and improves company culture.

i. Companies are implementing bias-free hiring practices.

ii. Employee resource groups (ERGs) are supporting underrepresented talent.

iii. Organizations are embedding DEI strategies into leadership development programs.

Workplaces that champion inclusivity will attract top-tier talent and strengthen their employer brand in the global market.

5. The Role of Employee Well-Being and Mental Health

As workplace expectations evolve, so too does the focus on employee well-being. Businesses are realizing that a burnt-out workforce is neither productive nor sustainable.

i. Mental health support programs are becoming standard corporate benefits.

ii. Companies are encouraging work-life balance through wellness initiatives.

iii. Leadership styles are shifting toward empathy, coaching, and emotional intelligence.

A workforce that feels valued and supported will be more engaged, loyal, and highly performing.

6. The Rise of Sustainability and Purpose-Driven Work

Today's employees—especially Millennials and Gen Z—seek purpose-driven work. They want to contribute to organizations that align with their values and take meaningful action on social and environmental issues.

    i. Companies are adopting sustainability goals and corporate social responsibility (CSR) initiatives.

    ii. Employees are prioritizing job roles that contribute to positive societal change.

    iii. Businesses that fail to address climate change and social issues may struggle with talent retention.

Organizations that integrate purpose into their business models will not only attract top talent but also enhance brand loyalty and stakeholder trust.

Preparing for the Workforce for Tomorrow

The future of work is dynamic, diverse, and digitally driven. Businesses must proactively adapt to these shifts by fostering a culture of continuous learning, flexibility, inclusivity, and well-being. Those that embrace change with open arms will cultivate a resilient workforce—one that is ready to navigate the challenges and opportunities of tomorrow.

Redefining Leadership in a Digital-First Workplace

The first digital workplace is transforming how businesses operate, collaborate, and compete. Traditional leadership models that relied on in-person management, rigid hierarchies, and slow decision-making are no longer effective in today's fast-paced, technology-driven environment. Modern enterprise leaders must embrace agility, digital fluency, and a people-centric approach to thrive in an era where remote work, automation, and data-driven decision-making are the new normal.

Successful leaders in digital-first organizations are not just managers, they are strategic enablers, fostering innovation, collaboration, and resilience in a distributed workforce. Mastering change in leadership requires adapting to new technologies, redefining workplace culture, and leading teams with a blend of empathy, decisiveness, and digital expertise.

1. The Shift to Digital-First Leadership

The modern business landscape has undergone a dramatic transformation, driven by advancements in cloud computing, artificial intelligence, and collaboration tools. This shift requires leaders to move away from traditional top-down leadership models and embrace digital-first strategies that enable flexibility, real-time decision-making, and seamless communication.

Key Changes in Leadership for a Digital-First World

i. **Data-Driven Decision-Making:** Leaders must leverage analytics and AI to make informed, agile decisions.

ii. **Remote and Hybrid Work Enablement:** Managing distributed teams requires new tools, strategies, and trust-based leadership.

iii. Continuous Learning and Digital Upskilling: Leaders must stay ahead of emerging technologies to guide their organizations effectively.

iv. Customer-Centric Mindset: Digital transformation enables hyper-personalization, requiring leaders to focus on customer experience like never before.

The digital-first approach demands a fundamental rethinking of leadership priorities, emphasizing adaptability and proactive transformation.

2. Leading with Agility and Innovation

A digital-first workplace thrives on rapid experimentation, real-time feedback, and continuous innovation. Leaders must cultivate an environment that encourages risk-taking, creative problem-solving, and cross-functional collaboration.

Best Practices for Agile Leadership

i. Embrace a Growth Mindset: Encourage teams to experiment, iterate, and learn from failures.

ii. Foster a Culture of Psychological Safety: Enable employees to voice ideas and concerns without fear of judgment.

iii. Adopt Agile Decision-Making Frameworks: Use iterative planning and real-time data to respond to market changes quickly.

iv. Leverage AI and Automation: Streamline workflows, enhance productivity, and free employees for higher-value work.

Agile leadership ensures that businesses remain resilient and adaptable in an ever-changing digital economy.

3. Building and Managing High-Performing Virtual Teams

Remote and hybrid work models are now permanent fixtures in the corporate world. Leaders must develop strategies to maintain productivity, engagement, and culture in a decentralized environment.

Strategies for Leading Distributed Teams Effectively

i. Invest in Digital Collaboration Tools: Utilize platforms like Slack, Microsoft Teams, and Zoom for seamless communication.

ii. Prioritize Outcome-Based Performance Metrics: Shift from hours-based management to results-driven evaluation.

iii. Enhance Virtual Employee Engagement: Regular check-ins, virtual team building, and recognition programs keep teams motivated.

iv. Create Clear Digital Workflows: Establish transparent processes that ensure accountability and efficiency in remote settings.

Leading high-performing virtual teams requires a balance of structure, flexibility, and trust.

4. The Evolving Role of Emotional Intelligence in Digital Leadership

In a digital-first environment, emotional intelligence (EQ) is just as critical as technical expertise. Leaders who can inspire, connect, and empathize with their teams, especially in virtual settings, drive stronger performance, retention, and innovation.

Core EQ Skills for Digital Leaders

i. Active Listening: Be fully present in digital conversations and ensure employees feel heard.

ii. Empathy and Inclusivity: Recognize the diverse challenges employees face in remote and hybrid work.

iii. Adaptability to Change: Maintain composure and resilience in times of disruption and uncertainty.

iv. Clear and Transparent Communication: Use digital channels effectively to articulate vision, goals, and expectations.

By mastering emotional intelligence, leaders can create a more cohesive, engaged, and high-performing digital workforce.

Leadership Reimagined for the Digital Age

The future of leadership is not about commanding from the top—it's about enabling teams to thrive in an interconnected, digital-first world. Business leaders who adapt to these new realities, embrace technology, and lead with agility and emotional intelligence will position their organizations for sustained success.

Mastering change in enterprise leadership means redefining the way leaders inspire, manage, and drive results in a landscape where technology and people must work in harmony.

Technology and Human Capital: Finding the Right Balance

In today's business landscape, organizations are constantly challenged to integrate cutting-edge technology while maintaining the value of human capital. As automation, artificial intelligence, and digital transformation reshape industries, leaders must strike a balance—leveraging technology to drive efficiency while fostering a workforce that remains engaged, innovative, and adaptable.

The Role of Technology in Business Evolution

Technology has become an indispensable force in modern enterprises. From AI-driven analytics to robotic process automation, businesses are using technology to streamline operations, reduce costs, and enhance decision-making. However, an over-reliance on automation without considering human expertise can lead to unintended consequences, such as reduced creativity, weakened employee morale, and resistance to change.

The Human Element: Why People Still Matter

Despite technological advancements, human intuition, critical thinking, and problem-solving remain irreplaceable. While machines can process vast amounts of data, it takes human insight to interpret results, make strategic decisions, and build meaningful relationships. Employees who are empowered to work alongside technology rather than being replaced by it can drive greater innovation and adaptability.

Achieving the Right Balance

Organizations that succeed in mastering change recognize that technology and human capital must complement each other. Key strategies include:

> **i. Reskilling and Upskilling** – Investing in employee training to ensure that workers can effectively collaborate with new technologies.
>
> **ii. Human-Centered Automation** – Implementing automation in a way that enhances human productivity rather than eliminating jobs.
>
> **iii. Agile Workforce Strategies** – Encouraging flexibility and continuous learning to help employees adapt to technological shifts.

Moving Forward

The businesses that will thrive in the future are those that see technology as an enabler rather than a replacement for human talent. By integrating digital tools with a people-first approach, organizations can foster a culture of innovation while maintaining a skilled and motivated workforce. The key to mastering change lies in embracing both the efficiencies of technology and the irreplaceable value of human expertise.

Preparing for Jobs That Don't Exist Yet

The pace of technological innovation is redefining industries at an unprecedented rate. Automation, AI, and digital transformation are not just altering how we work—they are reshaping the very nature of work itself. Many of the roles that will drive future economies have yet to be created, and professionals, businesses, and leaders must develop strategies to stay ahead of these shifts. The challenge isn't just keeping up with change, it's preparing for a future that is constantly being rewritten.

The Unpredictable Nature of Work Evolution

Throughout history, technological advancements have introduced new professions while rendering others obsolete. Just a decade ago, careers in blockchain, AI ethics, and cloud security were barely on the radar. Today, they are among the most in-demand roles. As emerging technologies accelerate this trend, businesses must foster a culture of adaptability to ensure they are not caught off guard by the next wave of change.

Building a Workforce with Future-Proof Skills

Since it's impossible to predict every new role that will emerge, organizations and individuals must prioritize skills that transcend specific job functions. Creativity, critical thinking, complex problem-solving, and adaptability will be the defining traits of professionals who thrive in the unknown. Businesses should focus on continuous learning initiatives, offering employees access to upskilling programs, mentorship, and real-world applications of emerging technologies.

Bridging Innovation and Human Potential

While automation and AI are reshaping industries, human ingenuity remains irreplaceable. The most successful businesses will be those that strike a balance between technological advancement and human expertise. Leaders must cultivate environments where experimentation, cross-disciplinary collaboration, and new ideas are encouraged—ensuring that employees are not just adapting to change but driving it.

Anticipating Industry Shifts and Creating Opportunities

Organizations that wait for disruption to happen will always be playing catch-up. Instead of reacting to industry shifts, forward-thinking companies invest in research, market analysis, and trend forecasting to anticipate what's next. This proactive mindset allows businesses to not only prepare for new jobs but also shape them, creating roles that align with both technological advancements and evolving consumer needs.

Embracing the Unknown with Confidence

Mastering change means accepting that the future of work will always be uncertain. The leaders and professionals who thrive will remain open to new possibilities, continuously develop their skills, and foster innovation within their organizations. By embracing change as an opportunity rather than a challenge, businesses and individuals can prepare for jobs that don't exist yet—and, in many cases, be the ones to create them.

MARIE TONGS

CHAPTER SEVEN
ETHICAL CHALLENGES IN A CHANGING BUSINESS LANDSCAPE

As businesses navigate rapid technological advancements, shifting consumer expectations, and evolving regulatory landscapes, ethical decision-making has become a defining factor in long-term success. In an era where corporate actions are scrutinized more than ever, mastering change requires enterprises to embed ethical considerations into their strategies, operations, and leadership practices.

From data privacy concerns and AI bias to environmental responsibility and corporate transparency, organizations must balance profitability with ethical responsibility. Those that proactively address ethical challenges not only mitigate risk but also build trust, foster innovation, and create lasting value for stakeholders.

1. The New Ethical Imperative: Balancing Profit and Responsibility

Ethics in business is no longer a secondary concern—it is a core component of strategy. Consumers, employees, and investors expect companies to take a stand on social, environmental, and governance issues. Leaders must navigate the complexities of maintaining profitability while ensuring ethical integrity.

Key Ethical Considerations for Business Leaders

i. Corporate Social Responsibility (CSR): Aligning business goals with social impact and sustainability efforts.

ii. Ethical Profitability: Ensuring business growth does not come at the expense of consumer rights, labor exploitation, or environmental harm.

iii. Stakeholder-Centric Decision-Making: Considering the long-term impact of business actions on employees, communities, and investors.

iv. Transparency and Accountability: Openly communicating policies, decisions, and challenges to build public trust.

Enterprises that embrace ethical leadership create resilient business models that withstand reputational risks and regulatory scrutiny.

2. Data Privacy, AI, and the Ethics of Digital Transformation

As companies leverage artificial intelligence (AI), big data, and automation to drive efficiency, they must also address the ethical concerns that accompany these advancements.

The Ethical Challenges of AI and Data-Driven Decision-Making

i. Bias in AI Models: Algorithms trained on biased data can reinforce discrimination in hiring, lending, and law enforcement.

ii. Data Privacy and Consumer Rights: Companies must ensure that personal data is collected, stored, and used responsibly.

iii. Automation and Workforce Displacement: Ethical considerations around job loss due to AI and robotic process automation (RPA).

iv. Algorithmic Transparency: The need for explainable AI to avoid "black box" decision-making that lacks accountability.

Leaders must develop ethical frameworks for AI governance, ensuring that technology serves humanity rather than undermines it.

3. Ethical Leadership in the Age of Transparency

With social media and digital connectivity amplifying corporate missteps, maintaining ethical leadership is no longer optional. Consumers and employees demand transparency, authenticity, and accountability from the organizations they support.

Principles of Ethical Leadership

i. Lead by Example: Executives and managers must model ethical behavior in decision-making and communication.

ii. Cultivate a Speak-Up Culture: Encourage employees to report unethical practices without fear of retaliation.

iii. Align Incentives with Ethics: Reward ethical behavior rather than short-term financial gains at any cost.

iv. Engage with Stakeholders: Collaborate with regulators, communities, and customers to ensure fair and responsible business practices.

By embedding ethics into leadership practices, businesses can maintain credibility and inspire loyalty.

4. The Future of Business Ethics: Preparing for Emerging Challenges

Ethical challenges in business will continue to evolve as new technologies, market dynamics, and global crises emerge. Organizations must proactively anticipate and address these challenges to stay ahead of ethical risks.

Emerging Ethical Considerations

i. Sustainability and Climate Responsibility: Companies will face growing pressure to meet environmental, social, and governance (ESG) goals.

ii. Digital Ethics in the Metaverse and Web3: New technologies will introduce concerns about digital identity, ownership, and misinformation.

iii. Ethical AI Regulations: Governments will increasingly regulate AI use, requiring businesses to adapt.

iv. Global Supply Chain Ethics: Companies will need to ensure fair labor practices and sustainability across international operations.

By fostering an ethical-first mindset, organizations can master change and lead with integrity in an unpredictable business environment.

Ethics as a Competitive Advantage

In a rapidly changing business landscape, ethics is not just a compliance requirement, it is a competitive advantage. Companies that prioritize ethical decision-making build trust, drive innovation, and create sustainable success. By integrating ethics into leadership, technology, and corporate strategy, businesses can navigate uncertainty with confidence and resilience.

The Ethics of AI, Automation, and Big Data

As businesses increasingly rely on AI, automation, and big data, ethical considerations have become central to responsible innovation. While these technologies offer immense potential for efficiency, productivity, and decision-making, they also raise critical concerns about privacy, bias, transparency, and accountability. Mastering change in the business world requires organizations to not only adopt these tools but to do so in a way that aligns with ethical principles and public trust.

The Power and the Pitfalls of AI and Automation

AI and automation have transformed industries by enhancing efficiency, reducing costs, and improving accuracy. However, they also introduce ethical risks:

>   **i. Bias in AI Decision-Making** – AI systems learn from data, and if that data contains biases, the outcomes can be discriminatory, leading to unfair hiring practices, lending decisions, or law enforcement actions.
>
>   **ii. Job Displacement** – While automation increases productivity, it can also replace human jobs. Ethical businesses must consider how to reskill workers and create new opportunities rather than simply cutting costs through automation.
>
>   **iii. Transparency and Explainability** – Many AI-driven decisions, especially in areas like finance or healthcare, impact people's lives. Yet, complex algorithms often operate as "black boxes," making it difficult to understand how decisions are made.

Big Data: A Double-Edged Sword

Big data fuels AI and automation, offering businesses deep insights into customer behavior, market trends, and operational efficiencies. However, ethical challenges emerge when organizations misuse or mishandle data:

>   **i. Privacy Violations** – Many companies collect massive amounts of personal data, often without users fully

understanding how their information is used. Stricter data regulations, such as GDPR and CCPA, now hold businesses accountable.

ii. Data Security Risks – Cybersecurity breaches have become a growing concern, with sensitive customer and corporate data increasingly targeted by hackers. Ethical organizations must invest in strong security measures to protect stakeholders.

iii. Informed Consent and Transparency – Ethical data usage requires businesses to clearly inform users about what data is being collected and how it will be used.

Building Ethical AI and Data Practices

For business leaders, mastering change in the digital era means embedding ethics into AI, automation, and big data strategies. Best practices include:

i. Ensuring Diversity in AI Development – Diverse teams help reduce bias in AI models by offering multiple perspectives on data collection and algorithm design.

ii. Prioritizing Transparency – Companies should strive to make AI decisions more explainable, providing clear insights into automated processes.

iii. Adopting Responsible Data Governance – Businesses should adhere to ethical data collection, storage, and sharing practices, ensuring compliance with regulations and user trust.

iv. Reskilling and Workforce Transition Planning – As automation reshapes industries, organizations should actively invest in reskilling employees to take on new roles in a tech-driven world.

The Future of Ethical AI and Data Use

As technology continues to evolve, the ethical considerations surrounding AI, automation, and big data will only become more complex. Businesses that proactively address these challenges—rather than reacting to public scrutiny or regulation—will position themselves as leaders in responsible innovation. Ultimately, organizations that prioritize ethics will build stronger relationships with customers, employees, and society at large, ensuring long-term success in an increasingly digital world.

Corporate Social Responsibility in a Fast-Moving World

In today's rapidly evolving business landscape, Corporate Social Responsibility (CSR) is no longer an optional initiative—it is an essential component of sustainable success. Consumers, investors, and employees increasingly expect organizations to go beyond profit-making and demonstrate a commitment to social and environmental well-being. However, as industries undergo digital transformation, economic shifts, and regulatory changes, businesses must continuously adapt their CSR strategies to remain relevant and impactful.

CSR as a Competitive Advantage

CSR is not just about philanthropy; it is a strategic advantage that can drive brand loyalty, enhance reputation, and create long-term value. Companies that actively engage in ethical business practices, environmental sustainability, and social impact initiatives are better positioned to attract customers and top talent. In an era where consumers align their purchasing decisions with their values, a well-integrated CSR approach can differentiate businesses in competitive markets.

Adapting to Changing Expectations

As societal concerns evolve, so do expectations for corporate responsibility. Issues such as climate change, diversity and inclusion, and ethical AI usage have become central to CSR discussions. Businesses must be proactive in addressing these concerns, ensuring that their policies, operations, and partnerships align with the shifting priorities of stakeholders. What worked five years ago may no longer be sufficient agility in CSR initiatives is key to maintaining credibility and relevance.

Technology's Role in CSR Evolution

Digital transformation and data analytics have made it easier for businesses to measure and report on their CSR efforts. Companies can now track carbon footprints, monitor supply chain ethics, and assess community impact with real-time data. AI-driven insights allow organizations to identify high-impact initiatives, predict social trends, and optimize their sustainability strategies. By leveraging technology, businesses can make CSR initiatives more transparent, accountable, and results driven.

Integrating CSR into Business Strategy

For CSR to be truly effective, it must be woven into the core business strategy rather than treated as a separate function. Companies that successfully integrate social responsibility into their operations—such as adopting sustainable sourcing, implementing fair labor practices, and supporting local communities—are more likely to achieve long-term profitability and resilience. Aligning CSR with business objectives ensures that social impact is not just a moral obligation but a driver of sustained growth.

The Future of CSR: Purpose-Driven Business

In a fast-moving world, CSR is no longer about checking boxes, it is about creating meaningful, measurable impact. Businesses that view social responsibility as an ongoing commitment rather than a static initiative will be the ones that thrive in the face of change. By staying agile, embracing innovation, and aligning CSR efforts with evolving global priorities, companies can foster trust, strengthen their brand, and contribute to a more sustainable and equitable future.

Transparency and Trust in the Age of Digital Business

In an era where businesses operate in a hyper-connected world, transparency is no longer optional, it's an expectation. The digital landscape has redefined how companies engage with customers, employees, and stakeholders, making trust one of the most valuable currencies in business. Organizations that embrace transparency and ethical business practices gain a competitive edge by fostering deeper relationships, enhancing brand reputation, and mitigating risks associated with misinformation, regulatory scrutiny, and consumer skepticism.

The Demand for Corporate Transparency

I. Consumer Expectations: Modern consumers demand honesty from brands, from product sourcing to pricing and data usage.

ii. Regulatory Pressures: Governments worldwide are introducing stricter disclosure laws for corporate governance, environmental impact, and data privacy.

iii. Investor Scrutiny: Shareholders prioritize transparency in financial reporting, executive compensation, and ESG (Environmental, Social, and Governance) initiatives.

iv. Workforce Accountability: Employees expect ethical leadership, clear communication, and fair workplace policies.

Companies that prioritize openness and integrity in their operations foster long-term loyalty and resilience in an unpredictable market.

Data Transparency and Digital Ethics

The digital economy thrives on data, but businesses must navigate the fine line between leveraging consumer information and protecting privacy. Mishandling data can lead to severe reputational damage and legal repercussions.

Key Transparency Challenges in the Digital Age:

i **Data Collection Practices:** Companies must be clear about what data they collect and how they use it.

ii. **AI Decision-Making:** Algorithmic transparency is crucial to prevent biased or unethical outcomes.

iii. **Cybersecurity and Privacy Compliance:** Businesses must proactively protect user information to avoid breaches and regulatory penalties.

iv. **Misinformation and Corporate Responsibility:** Companies must ensure ethical digital marketing and social media practices to prevent the spread of misleading content.

By implementing robust data governance frameworks and prioritizing ethical AI, organizations can strengthen trust and demonstrate accountability.

Building a Trust-First Business Model

Trust is not given, it is earned through consistent, ethical decision-making and clear communication. Businesses that proactively share information, address concerns openly, and take responsibility for their actions are better positioned to thrive.

Strategies for Fostering Trust in Digital Business:

i. Open Communication: Transparent leadership fosters confidence among employees and stakeholders.

ii. Authenticity in Branding: Companies that stay true to their values resonate more deeply with consumers.

iii. Third-Party Verification: Independent audits and certifications reinforce credibility in areas like sustainability and corporate governance.

iv. Proactive Crisis Management: Quickly acknowledging and addressing challenges builds confidence rather than eroding trust.

Transparency and trust are the foundation of long-term business resilience. In a world where digital interactions shape reputation and influence success, companies that master ethical business practices will lead the future.

Navigating Regulatory Changes and Compliance Risks

In today's fast-changing business landscape, regulatory compliance is no longer just a legal necessity, it's a strategic imperative. As global regulations evolve to keep pace with technological advancements, data privacy concerns, and ethical business practices, companies must master the art of adapting to new legal frameworks. Failure to do so can result in hefty fines, reputational damage, and operational disruptions.

The Ever-Changing Regulatory Landscape

Governments and regulatory bodies worldwide are constantly updating laws to address emerging risks. Key areas of concern include:

i. Data Privacy and Protection – Regulations like GDPR (General Data Protection Regulation) in Europe and CCPA (California Consumer Privacy Act) have redefined how businesses collect, store, and use customer data. Companies must ensure compliance or face severe penalties.

ii. AI and Automation Regulations – As AI adoption grows, so do concerns about bias, accountability, and transparency. Proposed laws, such as the EU's AI Act, aim to set guidelines for responsible AI deployment.

iii. Environmental, Social, and Governance (ESG) Compliance – Businesses are increasingly required to disclose their impact on sustainability and social responsibility, with regulations mandating transparent reporting.

iv. Industry-Specific Laws – Sectors like finance, healthcare, and technology face unique regulatory challenges that demand specialized compliance strategies.

Compliance as a Competitive Advantage

Rather than viewing compliance as a burden, leading organizations treat it as a differentiator. Companies that proactively align with regulations gain trust, improve operational efficiency, and mitigate legal risks. Strategies for mastering regulatory change include:

I. Building an Agile Compliance Framework – Businesses should establish flexible compliance programs that can quickly adapt to new laws and industry standards.

ii. Leveraging Technology for Compliance Management – AI-driven compliance tools can monitor regulatory changes, automate risk assessments, and ensure adherence to policies.

iii. Embedding Compliance into Company Culture – Training employees on regulatory best practices helps create a proactive compliance mindset across the organization.

The Risks of Non-Compliance

Ignoring or underestimating regulatory shifts can have severe consequences:

i. Financial Penalties – Violations of data protection laws or anti-competition regulations often result in multi-million-dollar fines.

ii. Operational Disruptions – Failure to comply with new industry mandates can lead to product recalls, shutdowns, or licensing revocations.

iii. Reputational Damage – Public trust is fragile; companies that neglect compliance may suffer irreversible brand harm.

Future-Proofing Compliance Strategies

To stay ahead, businesses must adopt a forward-thinking approach to regulatory adaptation:

i. Continuous Monitoring and Legal Expertise – Keeping track of global policy changes ensures companies remain compliant in all markets they operate in.

ii. Cross-Functional Collaboration – Compliance should not be siloed within legal departments but integrated into decision-making across business units.

iii. Scenario Planning for Regulatory Shifts – Companies that anticipate potential legal changes can adjust their strategies before new laws take effect.

In an era of increasing regulation, businesses that master change by staying compliant will not only avoid risks but also build stronger relationships with customers, investors, and regulators. Compliance is no longer just about following rules, it's about shaping a business that thrives in a complex and evolving world.

MARIE TONGS

CHAPTER EIGHT
THE ROLE OF CLOUD, AI, AND DIGITAL INFRASTRUCTURE IN BUSINESS EVOLUTION

In today's fast-paced business world, digital transformation is no longer an option, it is a necessity. Organizations that embrace emerging technologies such as cloud computing, artificial intelligence (AI), and advanced digital infrastructure are better equipped to navigate uncertainty, scale operations efficiently, and maintain a competitive edge. These technologies are not just enablers of productivity; they are redefining the way businesses operate, innovate, and deliver value.

Cloud Computing: The Foundation of Modern Business

Cloud technology has revolutionized business operations by providing scalable, flexible, and cost-effective solutions for data storage, computing power, and software deployment. Companies can now rapidly deploy applications, analyze vast amounts of data, and collaborate seamlessly across global teams—all without the limitations of on-premise infrastructure.

i. The shift to cloud-based solutions offers significant advantages, including

ii. Agility and scalability – Businesses can scale resources up or down based on demand, ensuring operational efficiency.

iii. Cost efficiency – Cloud models reduce the need for expensive hardware and maintenance, enabling businesses to optimize IT spending.

iv. Security and compliance – Leading cloud providers offer robust security frameworks and compliance tools to help organizations safeguard their data.

As businesses continue to embrace hybrid and multi-cloud strategies, the focus is shifting from mere adoption to optimizing cloud environments for maximum performance and innovation.

Artificial Intelligence: Transforming Decision-Making and Automation

AI is rapidly reshaping industries by enabling smarter decision-making, automating repetitive tasks, and uncovering insights from vast datasets. From predictive analytics to intelligent automation, businesses are leveraging AI to drive efficiency, personalize customer experiences, and enhance innovation.

Key areas where AI is making a significant impact include:

i. Predictive analytics – AI-driven models help businesses anticipate market trends, customer behavior, and operational risks.

ii. Process automation – From chatbots handling customer inquiries to AI-powered fraud detection in finance, automation is streamlining operations.

iii. Enhanced customer engagement – AI-driven personalization enables businesses to deliver more targeted and relevant experiences to customers.

However, as AI adoption accelerates, organizations must also address ethical concerns, data bias, and regulatory challenges to ensure responsible AI implementation.

Digital Infrastructure: The Backbone of Business Resilience

A strong digital infrastructure is the foundation of a modern enterprise. It encompasses everything from cloud-based networks and cybersecurity frameworks to real-time data processing and edge computing. Businesses that invest in resilient digital infrastructure can adapt more quickly to disruptions, minimize downtime, and support remote and hybrid workforces.

Core components of a future-proof digital infrastructure include:

i. Cybersecurity – With the rise of cyber threats, businesses must prioritize secure architectures and real-time threat detection.

ii. Edge computing – Processing data closer to the source (e.g., IoT devices) reduces latency and improves efficiency for real-time applications.

iii. Connectivity and 5G – Faster and more reliable networks enhance digital experiences and support new business models.

As digital infrastructure evolves, businesses must continuously assess their technological landscape, ensuring they remain agile and prepared for future disruptions.

Embracing Change: The Digital-First Mindset

For organizations to thrive in an era of rapid technological change, adopting a digital-first mindset is crucial. This means:

i. Encouraging a culture of continuous learning and innovation.

ii. Investing in technology that aligns with long-term business goals.

iii. Staying adaptable to emerging trends and market shifts.

The integration of cloud, AI, and digital infrastructure is not just about upgrading technology, it's about reimagining how businesses operate and compete. Those that master these changes will be positioned as industry leaders, ready to harness the full potential of digital transformation.

Why Digital Transformation Is No Longer Optional

In today's hyper-competitive business environment, digital transformation has shifted from being a strategic advantage to a fundamental necessity. Organizations that fail to modernize risk falling behind as industries embrace cloud computing, artificial intelligence (AI), and automation to drive efficiency, scalability, and innovation. The digital era demands agility, resilience, and a willingness to evolve in response to market dynamics and technological advancements.

The Acceleration of Digital Transformation

The past decade has seen an unprecedented acceleration in digital adoption across industries. Several key drivers are pushing businesses toward full-scale digital transformation:

> **i. The Rise of Cloud Computing:** Businesses are increasingly migrating to the cloud for cost efficiency, scalability, and flexibility. Cloud-based platforms allow seamless collaboration, enhanced security, and real-time data access.
>
> **ii. AI and Machine Learning Integration:** Organizations leverage AI-powered insights to optimize decision-making, enhance customer experiences, and automate processes that were previously labor-intensive.
>
> **iii. Automation and Process Optimization:** Robotic process automation (RPA) and intelligent workflows reduce operational bottlenecks, improve efficiency, and minimize human error.
>
> **iv. Evolving Customer Expectations:** Digital first experiences have become the standard, requiring businesses to adopt omnichannel strategies, hyper-personalization, and instant service delivery.

The businesses that proactively embrace digital transformation position themselves for long-term success, while those that resist risk becoming obsolete.

Overcoming Barriers to Digital Adoption

Despite its benefits, digital transformation comes with challenges that businesses must navigate:

> **i. Cultural Resistance:** Employees and leadership may resist change due to uncertainty, job displacement fears, or a lack of digital literacy.
>
> **ii. Legacy Infrastructure:** Outdated IT systems often create integration challenges, slowing down digital initiatives.
>
> **iii. Cybersecurity Concerns:** As businesses move to the cloud and automate processes, they must strengthen security measures to protect against cyber threats.
>
> **Iv. Investment Constraints:** Digital transformation requires financial commitment, and some organizations struggle to justify the return on investment (ROI).

Leaders must develop a structured digital strategy, invest in training, and ensure alignment between technology initiatives and business objectives to overcome these barriers.

The Business Case for Digital Transformation

Investing in digital transformation is not just about staying relevant, it's about unlocking new opportunities for growth, innovation, and efficiency. Some of the key benefits include:

> **i. Enhanced Agility:** Businesses can pivot faster in response to market shifts, disruptions, and emerging opportunities.
>
> **ii. Data-Driven Decision-Making:** AI-powered analytics enable real-time insights, improving strategic planning and operational efficiency.
>
> **iii. Cost Savings and Scalability:** Cloud and automation reduce infrastructure costs while allowing businesses to scale operations without significant overhead.
>
> **Iv. Competitive Differentiation:** Organizations that innovate through digital capabilities gain a stronger market position and customer loyalty.

Digital transformation is no longer optional; it is the foundation for business resilience and long-term success in an evolving global economy. Companies that embrace change and invest in digital capabilities today will define the future of their industries.

Building a Scalable and Secure Digital Infrastructure

In today's fast-paced business world, digital infrastructure is more than just a technical necessity—it's a strategic foundation for growth, innovation, and resilience. Businesses that fail to build scalable and secure technology systems risk falling behind, unable to adapt to evolving market demands, cybersecurity threats, and operational complexities. To master change, organizations must ensure their digital infrastructure is both flexible and fortified, enabling them to scale efficiently while safeguarding critical assets.

The Need for Scalability in Digital Infrastructure

Scalability is the ability of a system to handle increasing workloads, users, and data without performance degradation. As companies expand, their digital infrastructure must grow with them. Key considerations include:

i. Cloud-Based Solutions – Cloud computing allows businesses to scale on demand, reducing the need for costly on-premises infrastructure. Platforms like AWS, Microsoft Azure, and Google Cloud offer flexibility to handle growth efficiently.

ii. Modular and Microservices Architecture – Breaking down applications into smaller, independent services enables faster scaling and adaptability to changes in demand.

iii. Automated Resource Management – AI-powered tools can dynamically allocate computing power, storage, and network resources to optimize performance and cost efficiency.

Security as a Cornerstone of Business Resilience

While scalability is crucial, security cannot be an afterthought. A robust security framework protects businesses from data breaches, system failures, and cyber threats. Essential strategies include:

i. Zero-Trust Security Models – This approach requires strict identity verification at every access point, reducing risks associated with unauthorized access.

ii. End-to-End Encryption – Encrypting data in transit and at rest ensures that sensitive information remains protected from cybercriminals.

iii. Proactive Threat Detection – AI and machine learning-driven security systems can identify and neutralize threats before they cause significant damage.

iv. Regular Security Audits and Compliance – Adhering to industry standards (e.g., ISO 27001, GDPR, HIPAA) ensures that businesses stay ahead of regulatory requirements and avoid legal pitfalls.

Balancing Flexibility and Stability

A scalable and secure digital infrastructure should be agile enough to support innovation while maintaining operational stability. To achieve this balance:

i. Adopt Hybrid and Multi-Cloud Strategies – Using multiple cloud providers or combining on-premise and cloud infrastructure ensures business continuity and reduces dependency on a single provider.

ii. Implement DevSecOps Practices – Integrating security into the development lifecycle prevents vulnerabilities from emerging later in the process.

iii. Invest in Disaster Recovery and Redundancy – Backup solutions, failover mechanisms, and business continuity planning help minimize downtime in case of system failures or cyberattacks.

The Future of Digital Infrastructure

As businesses navigate rapid technological change, emerging trends will shape the future of scalable and secure digital infrastructure:

i. Edge Computing – Processing data closer to the source reduces latency and enhances real-time decision-making.

ii. AI-Driven IT Operations – Intelligent automation will optimize infrastructure management, reducing the need for manual intervention.

iii. Quantum Computing Considerations – As quantum technology evolves, businesses must prepare for both new opportunities and security challenges.

By mastering change in digital infrastructure, enterprises can future proof their operations, enabling them to scale seamlessly while maintaining the highest standards of security and reliability. A well-architected digital foundation is not just a technical asset, but a competitive advantage in the modern business landscape.

Harnessing AI for Smarter Decision-Making

In the modern business landscape, data-driven decision-making has become a fundamental pillar of success. As enterprises navigate an increasingly complex and fast-changing world, artificial intelligence (AI) has emerged as a powerful tool for enhancing efficiency, optimizing operations, and fostering innovation. By leveraging AI, businesses can move beyond traditional analytics and intuition-based decision-making to a more precise, scalable, and predictive approach.

AI as a Catalyst for Efficiency

AI-powered automation is transforming enterprise operations by reducing human error, streamlining workflows, and optimizing resource allocation. From supply chain management to customer service, AI-driven solutions can analyze vast datasets in real time, providing insights that drive smarter and faster decisions. Key areas where AI enhances efficiency include:

i. Process automation – AI-driven bots and robotic process automation (RPA) handle repetitive tasks, freeing up employees to focus on strategic initiatives.

ii. Predictive maintenance – In industries like manufacturing and logistics, AI can forecast equipment failures before they occur, reducing downtime and maintenance costs.

iii. Operational optimization – AI algorithms assess data patterns to identify inefficiencies, enabling businesses to refine operations and maximize productivity.

AI and Strategic Innovation

AI is not just about improving existing processes—it's also a catalyst for innovation. Businesses that effectively harness AI can identify new opportunities, develop smarter products, and create more personalized customer experiences. Some key areas where AI drives innovation include:

i. Product development – AI-powered simulations and design tools help companies prototype and test products faster than ever before.

ii. Market intelligence – AI models analyze market trends, competitor strategies, and consumer behavior, allowing businesses to anticipate demand and adjust strategies accordingly.

iii. Hyper-personalization – AI-driven recommendation engines enable businesses to tailor products, services, and marketing efforts to individual customer preferences.

Overcoming AI Adoption Challenges

Despite its transformative potential, AI adoption comes with challenges, including data quality, ethical considerations, and workforce readiness. To fully leverage AI, enterprises must:

i. Ensure high-quality, unbiased data – AI models are only as good as the data they are trained on. Businesses must establish strong data governance practices to mitigate bias and inaccuracies.

ii. Develop AI literacy across teams – While AI tools automate decision-making, human oversight is still essential. Organizations must invest in training employees to work effectively alongside AI.

iii. Adopt responsible AI practices – Transparency, fairness, and accountability in AI decision-making are critical to building trust with customers, stakeholders, and regulators.

The Future of AI in Decision-Making

As AI technology continues to evolve, its role in enterprise decision-making will expand even further. Advances in generative AI, real-time analytics, and autonomous systems will enable businesses to operate with unprecedented agility and foresight. Organizations that embrace AI as a strategic enabler—rather than just a tool—will be better positioned to master change and stay ahead in an increasingly competitive world.

Cybersecurity and Data Privacy in a Connected World

Protecting Business Assets and Customer Data in an Era of Digital Risks

In a world where digital transformation is accelerating at an unprecedented rate, cybersecurity and data privacy have become critical business imperatives. As enterprises shift to cloud computing, AI-driven decision-making, and automation, the volume of data being generated, shared, and stored continues to grow exponentially. This interconnected landscape presents significant risks, from cyberattacks and data breaches to regulatory penalties and reputational damage. Organizations that fail to prioritize cybersecurity risk not only financial losses but also a severe erosion of customer trust.

The Growing Threat Landscape

The digital age has brought immense opportunities, but it has also opened the door to increasingly sophisticated cyber threats. Cybercriminals are leveraging AI, automation, and advanced phishing techniques to exploit vulnerabilities in business systems. Key threats include:

i. Ransomware Attacks: Malicious software encrypts business data, demanding payment for its release, disrupting operations, and causing financial losses.

ii. Data Breaches: Unauthorized access to sensitive customer or business data can lead to compliance violations, legal consequences, and reputational harm.

iii. Phishing and Social Engineering: Cybercriminals manipulate employees into revealing confidential information by passing security protocols.

Iv. Insider Threats: Employees, whether intentionally or unintentionally, can expose data to cyber risks through misconfigurations, negligence, or malicious intent.

Given the growing complexity of cyber threats, businesses must adopt a proactive and multi-layered approach to cybersecurity.

Building a Resilient Cybersecurity Strategy

To mitigate digital risks and protect critical assets, organizations must develop and implement robust cybersecurity strategies. Essential components include:

i. Zero Trust Security Model: Assume that threats exist both inside and outside the organization, requiring strict identity verification for every user and device attempting to access business systems.

ii. Data Encryption and Secure Storage: Encrypt sensitive data both in transit and at rest to prevent unauthorized access.

iii. AI-Powered Threat Detection: Leverage artificial intelligence and machine learning to identify unusual behavior, detect threats in real time, and automate responses to cyber incidents.

iv. Multi-Factor Authentication (MFA): Strengthen access control by requiring multiple forms of verification before granting access to critical systems.

v. Regular Security Audits and Penetration Testing: Continuously assess vulnerabilities and test security defenses to identify and mitigate potential weaknesses.

A proactive cybersecurity approach reduces the likelihood of attacks and ensures faster recovery when breaches occur.

Data Privacy and Compliance: Navigating Regulatory Challenges

Beyond cybersecurity threats, businesses must also navigate complex data privacy regulations designed to protect consumer information. Governments worldwide have introduced stringent data protection laws, such as:

i. **General Data Protection Regulation (GDPR):** Enforces strict data privacy requirements for organizations operating within the European Union (EU).

ii. **California Consumer Privacy Act (CCPA):** Grants California residents' greater control over their personal data.

iii. **China's Personal Information Protection Law (PIPL):** Regulates how businesses collect, store, and use personal data in China.

Failure to comply with these regulations can lead to substantial fines, legal action, and reputational damage. To stay compliant, businesses must:

i. **Adopt Transparent Data Policies:** Clearly communicate how customer data is collected, stored, and used.

ii. Enable Data Portability and User Control: Allow customers to access, modify, or delete their personal information upon request.

iii. Implement Data Anonymization Techniques: Reduce risks by ensuring that personal data cannot be traced back to individuals.

iv. Maintain Robust Data Governance: Establish clear policies on data classification, access control, and lifecycle management.

By integrating cybersecurity and data privacy into their digital strategies, organizations can build customer trust and ensure long-term business sustainability.

The Future of Cybersecurity in a Hyperconnected World

As businesses continue to embrace cloud computing, AI, and IoT (Internet of Things), the cybersecurity landscape will evolve. Future trends include:

i. AI-Driven Security Operations: AI will play a crucial role in automating threat detection and response.

ii. Blockchain for Data Security: Decentralized encryption techniques will enhance data integrity and reduce fraud.

iii. Quantum-Resistant Cryptography: As quantum computing advances, businesses will need new encryption methods to stay ahead of potential cyber threats.

iv. Greater Focus on Ethical AI and Privacy-Preserving Technologies: Organizations will need to balance innovation with responsible data practices.

Cybersecurity is no longer just an IT concern—it is a core business function that ensures resilience, continuity, and trust in an increasingly digital world. Organizations that embed security and privacy into their business models will not only mitigate risks but also gain a competitive edge in a marketplace where trust is a valuable currency.

MARIE TONGS

CHAPTER NINE
FROM LEGACY SYSTEM TO INTELLIGENT AUTOMATION

In the modern business landscape, organizations must navigate a critical transformation, from outdated legacy systems to intelligent automation. Legacy systems, once the backbone of enterprise operations, now pose significant challenges: they are costly to maintain, lack flexibility, and hinder agility in a rapidly evolving digital economy. The shift to intelligent automation—leveraging AI, machine learning, and process automation—enables businesses to operate with greater efficiency, scalability, and innovation.

The Burden of Legacy Systems

Many enterprises still rely on decades-old IT infrastructure that was built for a different era. These systems often suffer from:

i. High Maintenance Costs – Maintaining and updating outdated technology consumes significant resources, diverting investment from innovation.

ii. Lack of Integration – Legacy systems struggle to connect with modern cloud platforms, AI tools, and real-time data analytics, leading to inefficiencies.

iii. Security Risks – Older systems are more vulnerable to cyber threats and compliance challenges, putting sensitive business data at risk.

i. Limited Scalability – Traditional systems cannot easily scale to meet the demands of a growing enterprise or adapt to new business models.

The Shift to Intelligent Automation

To stay competitive, businesses must transition from legacy systems to intelligent automation, which integrates:

i. Robotic Process Automation (RPA) – Automating repetitive, rule-based tasks (e.g., invoice processing, data entry) to improve efficiency and reduce errors.

ii. Artificial Intelligence and Machine Learning – Using AI-driven insights to optimize decision-making, detect patterns, and enhance predictive analytics.

iii. Cloud-Based Platforms – Migrating from on-premise infrastructure to cloud environments for flexibility, cost savings, and seamless scalability.

iv. Low-Code and No-Code Solutions – Empowering business teams to build and modify applications without deep technical expertise, accelerating innovation.

Overcoming Resistance to Change

The transition from legacy systems to automation is not just a technological shift—it requires a change in mindset. Key strategies to drive adoption include:

i. Executive Buy-In and Leadership Commitment – Change must be championed from the top, with a clear vision for digital transformation.

ii. Workforce Enablement – Upskilling employees to work alongside AI and automation ensures a smooth transition without job displacement concerns.

iii. Phased Implementation Approach – Instead of replacing entire systems overnight, businesses should adopt a step-by-step migration strategy.

iv. Measuring Impact and ROI – Tracking cost savings, productivity improvements, and customer satisfaction ensures that automation delivers measurable value.

The Future: A Fully Automated, Intelligent Enterprise

As businesses progress in their automation journey, the end goal is an intelligent enterprise—one where AI-driven decision-making, seamless system integration, and continuous optimization drive competitive advantage. Emerging trends shaping this future include:

i. Hyper automation – The convergence of RPA, AI, and advanced analytics to automate end-to-end business processes.

ii. Autonomous Decision Systems – AI-driven platforms that make real-time business decisions with minimal human intervention.

iii. AI-Augmented Workforce – Employees and AI working collaboratively, where machines handle repetitive tasks while humans focus on strategic initiatives.

Organizations that successfully transition from legacy systems to intelligent automation will not only survive but thrive in a world where adaptability and efficiency define success. The future belongs to businesses that embrace change, harness automation, and reimagine how they operate.

The Cost of Clinging to Outdated Technology

In an era where digital transformation is a key driver of business success, many organizations still struggle with the decision to modernize their technology infrastructure. While legacy systems may feel familiar and stable, they often come with significant hidden costs that hinder efficiency, innovation, and long-term growth. Businesses that fail to embrace change risk falling behind their competitors and missing out on opportunities to leverage emerging technologies.

Operational Inefficiencies and Rising Maintenance Costs

Older technology often requires extensive maintenance, leading to increased operational costs. Many enterprises find themselves allocating a disproportionate share of their IT budgets to keeping outdated systems running instead of investing in new solutions. Some key challenges include:

i. High support costs – As vendors phase out support for outdated software, businesses must pay premium fees for maintenance or hire specialized (and often scarce) talent to manage legacy systems.

ii. Lack of integration – Older systems typically struggle to communicate with newer platforms, leading to inefficiencies, data silos, and manual workarounds.

iii. Downtime risks – Aging infrastructure is more prone to failures, which can result in costly downtime and disruptions to business operations.

Hindering Innovation and Scalability

Legacy systems were often designed for a different era of business needs, making them inflexible in today's fast-moving market. Companies that rely on outdated technology may struggle with:

i. Slow adaptability – Older systems lack the agility to support rapid changes in market demands, regulatory requirements, or customer expectations.

ii. Limited data capabilities – Modern businesses rely on real-time data analytics to drive decisions, but legacy systems may not support advanced data processing or AI-driven insights.

iii. Inability to scale – Many outdated systems were not designed to handle the volume and complexity of today's digital business environment, limiting growth potential.

Security and Compliance Risks

Cybersecurity threats are evolving at an unprecedented pace, and outdated technology is a prime target for attacks. Legacy systems often lack critical security updates and may not comply with current data protection regulations, exposing organizations to:

i. Increased vulnerability to cyberattacks – Older software may have unpatched security flaws that hackers can exploit.

ii. Regulatory non-compliance – Many industries have strict data protection and privacy laws, and failure to meet these standards can result in hefty fines and reputational damage.

iii. Data breaches and trust erosion – Customers and partners expect businesses to protect their data. A security incident caused by outdated technology can severely impact brand trust and customer loyalty.

The Strategic Imperative to Modernize

While modernization requires investment, the long-term benefits far outweigh the costs of maintaining legacy systems. Businesses that transition to cloud-based solutions, AI-driven analytics, and scalable digital platforms gain:

i. Enhanced efficiency and cost savings – Reducing manual processes and automating workflows improves productivity.

ii. Greater innovation potential – Modern technology enables businesses to experiment, adapt, and stay ahead of industry trends.

iii. Stronger security and compliance – Up-to-date systems help mitigate cybersecurity risks and ensure regulatory alignment.

Organizations that recognize the cost of clinging to outdated technology and take proactive steps to modernize will be better positioned to navigate change, drive innovation, and maintain a competitive edge in the digital economy.

Steps to a Successful Digital Modernization Strategy

How Businesses Can Transition from Legacy Systems to Modern Platforms

As technology advances at an unprecedented pace, businesses must evolve to remain competitive. Many organizations, however, are still operating on outdated legacy systems—rigid, costly, and unable to support the agility required in today's fast-moving digital economy. Transitioning to modern platforms is no longer optional; it is a strategic necessity for long-term growth and resilience.

A successful digital modernization strategy requires careful planning, execution, and alignment with business goals. The following steps provide a roadmap for enterprises looking to transform their IT infrastructure, improve efficiency, and drive innovation.

1. Assessing the Current State of Legacy Systems

Before embarking on a digital transformation journey, businesses must first evaluate their existing infrastructure. A thorough assessment will help determine which systems need upgrading, replacing, or integrating with modern solutions. Key considerations include:

i. System Performance & Scalability: Are legacy systems slowing down operations or struggling to support business growth?

ii. Security & Compliance Risks: Are outdated systems exposing the company to cybersecurity threats or regulatory non-compliance?

iii. Integration Challenges: Do legacy systems create data silos that hinder cross-functional collaboration and analytics?

iv. Cost of Maintenance: Are maintenance expenses increasing while system performance declines?

By conducting an in-depth audit, organizations can identify pain points, prioritize areas for improvement, and build a case for modernization.

2. Defining a Clear Digital Transformation Vision

A successful modernization strategy begins with a well-defined vision. This involves aligning technological upgrades with business objectives to ensure that modernization efforts drive value. Key steps include:

i. Setting Measurable Goals: Define KPIs that align with business priorities, such as reducing operational costs, improving customer experience, or increasing system agility.

ii. Gaining Executive Buy-In: Digital transformation must be championed by leadership to secure funding, resources, and organizational commitment.

iii. Fostering a Culture of Change: Employees must be engaged and prepared for the transition, with clear communication about how modernization benefits them.

By establishing a clear vision, businesses can ensure that modernization efforts remain focused and strategically aligned.

3. Choosing the Right Modernization Approach

Not all legacy systems need to be replaced outright. Depending on business needs and budget constraints, different approaches can be taken:

i. Rehosting ("Lift and Shift") – Moving legacy applications to cloud infrastructure without significant modifications.

ii. Replatforming – Migrating to a modern cloud environment while making some optimizations for better performance.

iii. Refactoring/Rearchitecting – Redesigning applications to take full advantage of cloud-native features like microservices and containerization.

iv. Rebuilding – Developing entirely new applications from scratch to replace outdated systems.

v. Replacing – Moving to commercial off-the-shelf (COTS) software solutions instead of custom-built legacy applications.

Selecting the right approach depends on factors such as business urgency, budget, and long-term scalability requirements.

4. Leveraging Cloud, AI, and Automation for Scalability

Modernization is not just about replacing old systems; it's about embracing emerging technologies to create a more agile, data-driven organization. Businesses should prioritize:

i. Cloud Adoption: Migrating to cloud-based infrastructure to enable scalability, flexibility, and cost efficiency.

ii. AI and Machine Learning: Automating decision-making, improving predictive analytics, and optimizing operations.

iii. Intelligent Automation: Using robotic process automation (RPA) and workflow automation tools to eliminate manual tasks and enhance efficiency.

Iv. API-First Architecture: Ensuring seamless integration between applications, platforms, and third-party services to prevent data silos.

By incorporating these technologies, enterprises can future proof their operations and drive continuous innovation.

5. Ensuring a Smooth Implementation and Change Management

One of the biggest challenges in digital modernization is resistance to change. Organizations must have a structured implementation plan to minimize disruption and ensure a smooth transition. Key best practices include:

> **i. Phased Rollout Strategy:** Implement modernization initiatives in stages to reduce risk and allow teams to adapt gradually.
>
> **ii. Comprehensive Training Programs:** Upskill employees to ensure they can effectively use new technologies.
>
> **iii. Change Management Leadership:** Appoint digital transformation leaders to drive adoption and address challenges proactively.
>
> **iv. Ongoing Monitoring and Optimization:** Continuously track system performance and user feedback to refine processes and maximize ROI.

By prioritizing a people-first approach, businesses can overcome resistance and accelerate digital adoption.

The Competitive Advantage of Digital Modernization

Modernizing legacy systems is no longer just an IT initiative, it is a business imperative. Companies that successfully transition to modern platforms gain:

i. Greater Agility: The ability to pivot quickly in response to market changes and emerging opportunities.

ii. Enhanced Security: Protection against cyber threats with up-to-date security frameworks and compliance measures.

iii. Operational Efficiency: Reduced downtime, lower maintenance costs, and improved system performance.

iv. Data-Driven Decision-Making: Real-time analytics and AI-driven insights to drive smarter business strategies.

Enterprises that embrace digital modernization will not only stay ahead of competitors but also build a resilient foundation for future growth in an increasingly digital world.

AI-Driven Automation: Efficiency, Speed, and Scalability

In today's fast-paced business environment, organizations must constantly evolve to stay competitive. AI-driven automation has emerged as a powerful tool to enhance efficiency, accelerate processes, and scale operations with minimal human intervention. From streamlining workflows to optimizing decision-making, AI-powered automation is reshaping how enterprises operate, making them more agile and resilient in the face of change.

Boosting Efficiency Through Intelligent Automation

Traditional automation focuses on predefined rules and repetitive tasks, but AI-driven automation takes it a step further. By incorporating machine learning, natural language processing, and advanced analytics, businesses can:

> i. Reduce Manual Workload – AI systems can handle high-volume, repetitive tasks such as data processing, document analysis, and customer support, freeing employees for higher-value work.
>
> ii. Enhance Accuracy and Consistency – Unlike manual processes prone to errors, AI-driven automation ensures greater precision and compliance across operations.
>
> iii. Improve Decision-Making – AI analyzes large datasets in real time, identifying trends and anomalies that enable faster and more informed business decisions.

Accelerating Business Speed with AI

Speed is a critical factor in today's dynamic business landscape. AI-driven automation allows companies to move faster by:

> **i. Automating Customer Interactions** – AI chatbots and virtual assistants provide instant responses, reducing wait times and enhancing customer satisfaction.

ii. Optimizing Supply Chains – Predictive analytics and automated logistics help businesses anticipate demand fluctuations, manage inventory, and streamline distribution.

iii. Real-Time Fraud Detection – AI-powered security systems monitor transactions and detect suspicious activity within milliseconds, protecting businesses from cyber threats.

Scaling Operations Seamlessly with AI

As businesses grow, manual processes become bottlenecks that limit scalability. AI-driven automation enables enterprises to scale effortlessly by:

i. Handling Increased Workloads – AI systems can process vast amounts of data without requiring additional human resources, ensuring smooth expansion.

ii. Personalizing Customer Experiences at Scale – AI-driven marketing automation can segment audiences, tailor recommendations, and optimize customer journeys across millions of users.

iii. Managing Workforce Flexibility – Automated HR and workforce management tools streamline hiring, training, and employee engagement, ensuring a productive and adaptable workforce.

The Future of AI-Driven Automation in Business

The adoption of AI-driven automation is no longer optional—it is a strategic necessity. As businesses continue to integrate AI into their core operations, we can expect:

    i. Hyperautomation – The fusion of AI, robotic process automation (RPA), and data analytics to create fully autonomous business processes.

    ii. AI-Augmented Decision-Making – AI will act as a strategic partner, providing insights and recommendations that help leaders make data-driven decisions.

    iii. Human-AI Collaboration – AI will not replace human expertise but will enhance productivity by allowing professionals to focus on creative problem-solving and strategic planning.

AI-driven automation is revolutionizing the way businesses operate, delivering unparalleled efficiency, speed, and scalability. Organizations that embrace this transformation will gain a competitive edge, driving innovation and resilience in an ever-changing marketplace.

Overcoming Resistance to Change in Digital Transformation

Digital transformation is no longer a luxury; it's a necessity for businesses striving to stay competitive in an evolving market. Yet, despite its clear benefits, organizations often encounter resistance when implementing new technologies or processes. Employees, managers, and even leadership can hesitate to embrace change due to uncertainty, fear of job displacement, or a lack of understanding. Successfully navigating this resistance is crucial for fostering innovation and ensuring long-term success.

Understanding the Root of Resistance

Resistance to change typically stems from a few common concerns:

i. Fear of Job Loss – Employees worry that automation and AI-driven solutions will replace their roles, leading to job insecurity.

ii. Lack of Digital Skills – Many workers feel unprepared to use new technologies and fear being left behind.

iii. Comfort with Familiar Processes – Long-standing workflows and legacy systems create a sense of stability, making change feel risky and unnecessary.

iv. Unclear Benefits – If employees don't understand the value of digital transformation, they may see it as additional work rather than an improvement.

V Lack of Trust in Leadership – A history of failed initiatives or poor communication can make employees skeptical about new changes.

Strategies to Overcome Resistance

1. Communicate the Vision Clearly

Transparency is key when implementing change. Leaders must clearly articulate:

i. Why the transformation is necessary – Link digital initiatives to business goals and competitive advantages.

ii. How it will impact employees – Address concerns head-on, explaining how technology will enhance roles rather than eliminate them.

iii. What success looks like – Provide a roadmap that includes short-term wins and long-term benefits.

2. Involve Employees Early

People are more likely to support change when they feel like active participants rather than passive recipients. Ways to encourage involvement include:

i. Seeking feedback on potential changes before implementation.

ii. Establishing cross-functional teams to pilot new technologies.

iii. Encouraging employees to contribute ideas for process improvements.

3. Invest in Upskilling and Reskilling

A workforce that feels empowered with new skills will be more open to transformation. Companies should:

i. Offer continuous training in digital tools and technologies.

ii. Provide mentorship and support for employees transitioning to new roles.

iii. Foster a growth mindset, emphasizing that learning is an ongoing process.

4. Foster a Culture of Innovation

To create a lasting shift in mindset, organizations must:

i. Encourage experimentation and reward employees for taking initiative.

ii. Normalize change by making adaptability part of the company's DNA.

iii. Highlight success stories of employees who have embraced new technologies and benefited from them.

5. Provide Strong Leadership and Support

Change must be championed from the top. Leaders should:

i. Lead by example by adopting new technologies themselves.

ii. Address concerns empathy, acknowledging employee fears while offering solutions.

iii. Set clear expectations and provide the necessary resources to ensure a smooth transition.

Embracing Change as a Competitive Advantage

Organizations that successfully overcome resistance to digital transformation don't just survive disruption, they thrive in it. By addressing workforce concerns, providing ongoing support, and fostering a culture of innovation, businesses can turn change from a challenge into a powerful advantage. The key is to make transformation a shared journey—one that employees and leaders navigate together with confidence and clarity.

CHAPTER TEN
BUILDING A FUTURE-PROOF CAREER IN A CONSTANTLY EVOLVING BUSINESS WORLD

The modern business landscape is defined by rapid technological advancements, shifting market dynamics, and evolving job roles. For professionals seeking long-term success, adaptability and continuous growth are essential. Future-proofing a career is no longer about mastering a single skill or industry, it's about cultivating a mindset of resilience, learning, and strategic reinvention.

This chapter explores the key principles for building a career that thrives amid uncertainty and change. Whether you are an executive, entrepreneur, or emerging professional, the ability to navigate transformation will determine your long-term success.

1. Embracing Lifelong Learning as a Career Strategy

The shelf life of skills is shrinking. As automation and AI reshape industries, professionals must commit to lifelong learning to stay relevant. This means:

    i. **Developing a Growth Mindset:** Viewing change as an opportunity rather than a threat.

ii. Continuous Upskilling: Investing in new skills that align with industry trends and future job demands.

iii. Leveraging Online Learning & Certifications: Using platforms like Coursera, LinkedIn Learning, and executive education programs to stay ahead.

iv. Building Multi-Disciplinary Knowledge: Combining expertise across different domains (e.g., business and technology) to increase career versatility.

Companies now value professionals who proactively learn and adapt. Future-proofing a career requires making learning an ongoing habit.

2. Developing Agility and Resilience in a Disruptive Workplace

With industries undergoing frequent transformations, professionals must cultivate agility and resilience. This involves:

i. Staying Ahead of Industry Trends: Following market shifts, emerging technologies, and new business models.

ii. Pivoting When Necessary: Being open to career transitions, whether shifting roles, industries, or business functions.

iii. Embracing Change Instead of Resisting It: Viewing workplace disruptions—such as automation or remote work—as opportunities to grow.

iv. Strengthening Emotional Intelligence (EQ): Building self-awareness, adaptability, and the ability to navigate workplace challenges effectively.

In an unpredictable business world, those who can pivot quickly will sustain long-term career growth.

3. Leveraging Digital Tools and Networking for Career Growth

Success is no longer just about "what you know, but also *who you know* and *how you leverage digital resources*. To future-proof a career, professionals should:

i. Enhance Their Digital Presence: Build a strong LinkedIn profile, share insights, and engage with industry leaders.

ii. Develop a Strategic Network: Connect with mentors, peers, and industry professionals to stay informed and uncover new opportunities.

iii. Utilize AI and Automation for Career Advancement: Leverage AI-driven learning platforms, career coaching tools, and digital productivity apps.

iv. Establish Thought Leadership: Write articles, speak at conferences, and position yourself as an expert in your field.

A well-connected professional with a strong digital presence is more likely to thrive in the evolving job market.

4. Futureproofing Through Innovation and Entrepreneurial Thinking

To remain competitive, professionals must think beyond traditional career paths and embrace innovation. This includes:

i. Adopting an Entrepreneurial Mindset: Whether working in a company or running a business, thinking like an entrepreneur fosters problem-solving and innovation.

ii. Identifying Emerging Opportunities: Being proactive in spotting trends and positioning yourself for new roles and industries.

iii. Developing Adaptable Leadership Skills: Leading teams through change, driving innovation, and fostering a culture of agility.

iv. Considering Multiple Career Pathways: Exploring side projects, consulting, or digital businesses as additional income streams.

By cultivating an innovative mindset, professionals can navigate uncertainty with confidence and create new opportunities for themselves.

The Future Belongs to Those Who Adapt

In a business world where disruption is constant, mastering change is the key to long-term career success. The most successful professionals are those who embrace learning, cultivate resilience, leverage digital tools, and continuously reinvent themselves.

The future of work is not about avoiding change, it's about mastering it.

Why Career Adaptability Matters More Than Ever

In an era defined by rapid technological advancements, shifting market demands, and evolving job roles, career adaptability is no longer optional, it is essential for survival and success. Professionals who embrace flexibility, continuous learning, and proactive skill development are the ones who thrive in uncertain environments.

The Acceleration of Change

Industries across the board are experiencing unprecedented transformations. Automation, AI, and digitalization are redefining job functions, making traditional skill sets obsolete faster than ever before. The ability to pivot, upskill, and embrace new challenges is what differentiates those who stay relevant from those who struggle to keep up.

The Rise of Non-Linear Career Paths

Gone are the days of predictable career trajectories. The modern professional must be prepared for lateral moves, career shifts, and even complete industry changes. The key to long-term success lies in cultivating a mindset that sees change as an opportunity rather than a threat.

Building a Future-Proof Skillset

Organizations now prioritize employees who can adapt, innovate, and work across disciplines. Soft skills such as critical thinking, communication, and problem-solving are just as crucial as technical expertise. Those who actively engage in lifelong learning and invest in professional development will have a competitive edge.

Embracing a Growth Mindset

Adaptability is not just about acquiring new skills; it's about cultivating a mindset that embraces change. Professionals who see disruptions as opportunities for growth rather than obstacles are more likely to excel in dynamic business landscapes.

As industries continue to evolve, the professionals who master change will be the ones leading the future. Career adaptability is no longer a luxury, it's the foundation of success in an unpredictable world.

Networking, Personal Branding, and Digital Presence

In today's fast-moving business landscape, success is no longer just about what you know, it's also about who you know and how you present yourself. As industries evolve and digital transformation reshapes the way professionals operate, networking, personal branding, and maintaining a strong digital presence have become essential for career resilience. Whether you're an entrepreneur, an executive, or a rising professional, strategically managing your professional image and connections can open doors to new opportunities, collaborations, and long-term stability.

The Power of Networking in a Changing Business World

Networking has always been a key driver of professional success, but in an era of rapid change, its importance has only grown. Strong professional networks provide:

i. Access to Opportunities – Many career advancements and business deals happen through referrals and personal connections rather than job applications or cold outreach.

ii. A Safety Net During Uncertainty – In times of industry disruption or economic downturns, a well-established network can provide new job leads, business partnerships, or mentorship.

iii. Fresh Insights and Learning – Engaging with industry peers allows professionals to stay informed about market trends, emerging technologies, and best practices.

To build and maintain a strong network:

i. Engage in Industry Events – Attend conferences, seminars, and professional meetups to connect with like-minded professionals.

ii. Nurture Existing Relationships – Don't just reach out when you need something; regularly check in with colleagues and offer value to your network.

iii. Join Online Communities – LinkedIn groups, professional forums, and social media platforms provide excellent opportunities to interact with industry leaders and influencers.

Building a Strong Personal Brand

Your personal brand is your professional reputation, how people perceive you and the value you bring. In a world where first impressions often happen online, a well-crafted personal brand can set you apart in a competitive market.

Key elements of a powerful personal brand include:

i. Clarity of Expertise – Clearly define your niche and area of expertise. Whether you're a data strategist, business transformation leader, or innovation consultant, ensure your brand communicates what you bring to the table.

ii. Authenticity and Consistency – Your brand should be an honest reflection of your skills, values, and experiences. Consistency across different platforms, your LinkedIn profile, personal website, and speaking engagements—builds credibility.

iii. Thought Leadership – Share insights, write articles, and engage in discussions that position you as a knowledgeable and forward-thinking professional in your field.

Leveraging Digital Presence for Influence and Visibility

A strong digital presence allows professionals to reach a wider audience, establish authority, and stay top-of-mind in their industry. Some strategies to enhance digital presence include:

    i. Optimizing LinkedIn – A complete and engaging LinkedIn profile, with a compelling summary, professional achievements, and regular activity, can attract career opportunities and connections.

    ii. Content Creation – Writing blog posts, publishing case studies, or hosting webinars can help demonstrate expertise and engage a broader audience.

    iii. Strategic Social Media Engagement – Actively participating in professional discussions on platforms like Twitter, Medium, and industry-specific forums can enhance visibility and influence.

Adapting for Long-Term Career Resilience

As industries continue to evolve, professionals who actively network, cultivate their personal brands, and maintain a strong digital presence will be better positioned to navigate change. The key is to remain adaptable, continually expand your professional circle, and ensure that your online and offline presence reflects your expertise and vision. In an unpredictable business world, a well-connected and well-branded professional will always have a competitive edge.

The Road Ahead: Preparing for a Future You Can't Predict

The only certainty in today's business world is change. Technological advancements, market disruptions, and shifting consumer behaviors make it impossible to predict the exact trajectory of any industry. However, professionals and organizations that embrace uncertainty as an opportunity—rather than a threat—will position themselves for long-term success.

To thrive in an unpredictable future, it is essential to develop the right mindset, strategies, and habits that allow for continuous reinvention. Here's how professionals can stay ahead in a business landscape that refuses to stand still.

1. Cultivating an Adaptive Mindset

The most successful leaders and professionals are not those who resist change, but those who embrace it. Developing an adaptive mindset requires:

> **i. Seeing Change as an Opportunity:** Rather than fearing disruptions, view them as moments to grow and innovate.
>
> **ii. Being Comfortable with Uncertainty:** Accept that the future is unpredictable and develop confidence in navigating ambiguity.
>
> **iii. Learning to Let Go of Outdated Strategies:** Clinging to old ways of doing business can lead to stagnation. Be willing to experiment and evolve.

iv. Focusing on Agility Over Perfection: In a rapidly changing world, speed and adaptability often outweigh rigid planning and over-analysis.

The ability to pivot quickly and seize new opportunities is a defining trait of future-ready professionals.

2. Developing a Continuous Learning Strategy

The future belongs to those who are willing to learn, unlearn, and relearn. As industries evolve, professionals must actively pursue knowledge to stay competitive. This involves:

i. Engaging in Lifelong Learning: Regularly updating skills through courses, certifications, and industry research.

ii. Diversifying Knowledge Areas: Expanding expertise beyond a single domain to increase career flexibility.

iii. Investing in Digital Literacy: Mastering emerging technologies such as AI, cloud computing, and automation to stay relevant.

iv. Learning from Failures and Feedback: Using setbacks as valuable learning experiences to refine strategies and decision-making.

A proactive approach to learning ensures that professionals remain indispensable, regardless of industry shifts.

3. Strengthening Your Professional Network

Success in a changing business world isn't just about what you know, it's about who you know. A strong network provides valuable insights, career opportunities, and collaborative possibilities. To build a resilient professional network:

> **i. Engage with Industry Leaders:** Follow and interact with thought leaders to stay informed about emerging trends.
>
> **ii. Join Professional Communities:** Participate in forums, associations, and business groups for knowledge-sharing and support.
>
> **iii. Prioritize Relationship-Building:** Develop meaningful professional connections rather than transactional interactions.
>
> **Iv Leverage Digital Platforms:** Use LinkedIn, industry webinars, and online communities to stay connected with the global workforce.

A well-established network serves as a safety net in times of change and uncertainty.

4. Creating a Personal and Professional Growth Plan

Preparing for an unpredictable future requires intentional action. Instead of passively reacting to change, professionals must proactively shape their career paths by:

i. Setting Clear Yet Flexible Goals: Define objectives but allow room for adjustments as industries shift.

ii. Exploring Alternative Career Paths: Consider new roles, industries, or entrepreneurial ventures that align with evolving business trends.

iii. Developing Leadership and Problem-Solving Skills: Strengthen the ability to guide teams and organizations through change.

iv. Embracing Experimentation: Be willing to test new ideas, take calculated risks, and step outside your comfort zone.

By actively designing a career roadmap that accounts for change, professionals can turn uncertainty into a strategic advantage.

Thriving in an Unpredictable Future

The future of business and enterprise is impossible to predict with complete certainty. However, those who prepare by cultivating adaptability, continuous learning, strategic networking, and proactive career planning will be well-positioned to thrive—no matter what changes arise.

In the face of uncertainty, the best strategy is not to resist change but to master it.

Embracing Change as Your Greatest Advantage

The business world will never stop evolving, neither should you. Mastering change is not about predicting the future with certainty; it's about preparing yourself to thrive no matter what the future holds. The most successful professionals and organizations are not those who resist disruption, but those who harness it to innovate, grow, and lead.

Embrace change with confidence. View challenges as opportunities. Invest in your growth, adapt with resilience, and cultivate a mindset that welcomes transformation. The future belongs to those who are ready to shape it.

The journey of mastering change never truly ends—but for those willing to take bold steps forward, the possibilities are limitless. Now, it's your turn to lead the way.

www.ingramcontent.com/pod-product-compliance
Lightning Source LLC
LaVergne TN
LVHW092007090526
838202LV00001B/36